SWITZ

GW01185194

By the staff of Editions Berlitz

How to use our guide

These 192 pages cover the **highlights** of Switzerland, grouped by area under twelve different headings. Although not exhaustive, our selection of sights will enable you to make the most of your holiday.

The **sights** to see are contained between pages 26 and 135. Those most highly recommended are pinpointed by the Berlitz traveller symbol.

The **Where to Go** section on p. 25 will help you plan your visit according to the time available.

For **general background** see the sections Switzerland and the Swiss p. 8, Facts and Figures p. 16 and History. p. 17.

Entertainment and **activities** (including eating out) are described between pp. 135 and 151.

The **practical information,** hints and tips you will need before and during your trip begin on page 15. This section is arranged alphabetically with a list for easy reference.

The **map section** at the back of the book (pp. 178–187) will help you find your way round and locate the principal sights.

Finally, if there is anything you cannot find, look in the complete **index** (pp. 188–192).

Text: Ken Bernstein
Layout: Doris Haldemann
Cartography: © Hallwag Ltd., Berne, Switzerland

We wish to express our thanks to the Swiss National Tourist Office in Zurich and to the regional offices throughout Switzerland, as well as to the Swiss Federal Railways. We are also grateful to Margaret Studer, Gérard Chaillon and Pierre-André Dufaux for their valuable assistance.

Printed in Switzerland by Weber S.A., Bienne.

CONTENTS

CONTENTS

Photos: Edmond van Hoorick, cover; Daniel Vittet pp. 8, 9, 21, 22, 25, 28, 30, 32, 35, 39, 41, 44, 53, 54, 57, 60, 61, 62, 66, 68, 73, 83, 86, 89, 90, 96, 139, 143, 149; Claude Huber pp. 11, 13, 18, 19, 47, 101, 102, 105, 109, 112, 114, 115, 117, 118, 121, 123, 124, 126, 127, 130, 132, 136, 137, 140, 142, 144, 147; Swissair pp. 76–7.

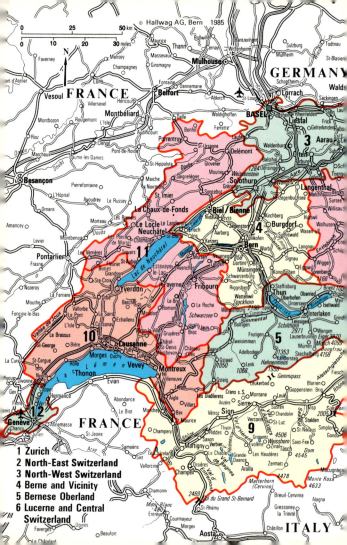

Hallwag AG, Bern 1985

GERMANY

FRANCE

BASEL

1 Zurich
2 North-East Switzerland
3 North-West Switzerland
4 Berne and Vicinity
5 Bernese Oberland
6 Lucerne and Central
Switzerland

ITALY

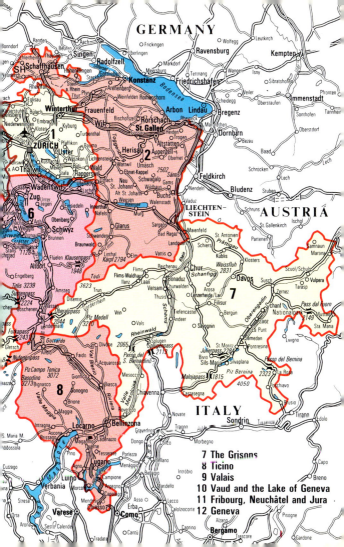

GERMANY

Randen
Beuren
Frickingen
Wolfegg
Leutkirch
Bonndorf
Thayngen
Überlingen
Ravensburg
Kempten
Singen
Radolfzell
Markdorf
SH
Schaffhausen
Hallemdingen
Meersburg
Tettnang
Isny
Sibratshofen
Eglisau
Steckborn
Konstanz
Friedrichshafen
Wangen
Pfronten
Rheinau
Arenenberg
Bodensee
Scheidegg
Oberstaufen
Immenstadt
Bülach
Thur
Weinfelden Romanshorn
Lindau
Bregenz
Sonthofen
Tannheim
Niederwenningen
Embrach
Winterthur
Frauenfeld
Bischofszell
Arbon
Rheineck
Dornbirn
Oberstdorf
Kloten
Kyburg
Wil
Hörschach
Heiden
Baad
Turbenthal
St. Gallen
Trogen
ZÜRICH
1
Pfäffikon
Bauma
Herisau
Appenzell
Altstätten
Lech
Uster
2
Oberriet
Feldkirch
Thalwil
Wald
Lichtensteig
Urnäsch
Säntis
Schrocken
Lech
Wädenswil
Rapperswil
Wattwil
2502
Schwägalp
Bludenz
Stuben
Zug
Einsiedeln
Neu St. Johann
Alt St. Johann
Gams
Buchs
Nendeln
6
Oberberg
Näfels
Weesen
Walenstadt
LIECHTEN-STEIN
Schwyz
Glarus
Sargans
Ischgl
Brunnen
Bad Ragaz
Maienfeld
St. Antonien
St. Gallenkirch
AUSTRIA
Schwanden
Landquart
Schiers
Prättigau
Partenen
Samnaun
Martina
Altdorf
Klausenpass
Linthal
Karpf 2794
Vattis
Reichenau
Kublis
Klosters
Scuol/Schuls
Vulpera
Titlis 3239
Tödi
Flims-Waldhaus
Chur
Weissfluh
2831
Davos
Susch
Surenenpass
3623
Ilanz
Laax
Schanfigg
7
Zernez
Sta. Maria
Göschenen
Trun
Versam
Chur
walden
Arosa
Oberengadin
Pass dal Fuorn
Müstair
Disentis
Vnin
Vals
Thusis
Lenzerheide/Lai
Filisur
Bergün
Zuoz
Nationalpark
2149
Faido
Olivone
Splügen
Tiefencastel
Savognin
Samedan
Pontresina
Livigno
8
Giornico
Biasca
Mesocco
Chiavenna
St. Moritz
Juterpass 2284
Bivio
Sils-Maria
Silvaplana
Passo del Bernina
Locarno
Bellinzona
Novate
Castasegna
Malojapass 1815
Piz Bernina
4050
2323
Poschiavo
Tirann
ITALY
Sondrio

7 The Grisons
8 Ticino
9 Valais
10 Vaud and the Lake of Geneva
11 Fribourg, Neuchâtel and Jura
12 Geneva

SWITZERLAND AND THE SWISS

Like a breath of fresh air, Switzerland revives sagging spirits. Pine forests scale steep mountainsides to the barrier of granite and eternal snow. Wild, thin waterfalls rush to feed mirror lakes. In the verdant valleys—some scarcely wider than ravines—bells clang as the fat, black and tan cows graze. Medieval castles survey villages brightened by paintbrush and flowerpot.

Those intriguing Swiss bank accounts may be numbered and hidden, but the nation's visible marvels are countless. And priceless.

Everything is squeezed into some 16,000 square miles; three Switzerlands would fit neatly into the area of England. And yet, for

a country so small, the variety is astonishing. The climate ranges from the subpolar of some of Europe's loftiest mountains to the near-Mediterranean — palm trees and all — in southernmost Ticino. Each part of the country, and sometimes each village, seems to have invented its own rules of architecture and decoration.

The variety of Switzerland is more than scenic. Deep cultural currents converge at this linguistic crossroads where the population is almost evenly divided into Catholics and Protestants. Three major European languages have official status here. Seventy-five per cent of the population speak

True to their traditions, the simple mountain folk remain the very essence of the Swiss nation.

Schwyzerdütsch, a dialect of German; 20 per cent claim French as their mother tongue, and 4 per cent, Italian. A fourth language, the exotic Romansh, is proudly preserved by about one per cent of the people, most of whom live in the Grisons, near the Austrian border. Switzerland has so many official names—Schweiz, Suisse, Svizzera, Svizra—that the coins and postage stamps have no room for all of them. So the Latin, *Helvetia*, is used.

Each group has its own traditions, literature, gastronomy and outlook on life, but a subtle and friendly interchange goes on, making Switzerland a lively patchwork of people and ideas. A grass-roots democratic system takes account of regional aspirations; the linguistic and religious divergences usually balance out in peaceful coalitions and compromises. Each of the cantons (states) enjoys considerable autonomy. So do the communes, more than 3,000 rural and municipal boroughs. But the real power belongs to the people: the instruments of popular initiative and referendum—descendants of the age-old Swiss town meeting—are frequently wielded locally and nationally to bring in new laws or torpedo old ones.

In the unpretentious federal capital at Berne, the oratory of some of Europe's lowest-paid legislators starts, Swiss style, early in the morning. Ultimate executive authority resides in a seven-member cabinet. The Swiss seem to prefer inconspicuous politicians to personality cults, and the presidency of the republic rotates every year. The head of state keeps such a low profile that many citizens would be hard-put to name the incumbent.

The modesty that veils public servants carries over to the rich and famous; at last count no fewer than 40,000 millionaires were resident in Switzerland. They are likely to be seen—or rather, not noticed—riding the trams, for the Swiss don't approve of flaunting wealth or status.

Ordinary people live well, too: the standard of living is enviably high by any international criterion. Moreover, this prosperity has been attained with few natural resources. In place of coal and oil, for instance, the Swiss harness the water power of their Alps. Raw materials imported into this landlocked country are transformed, with skilled labour and all-around ingenuity, into top quality, high-revenue exports. Swiss perfectionism and hard work make the difference.

Next year's wine starts with a bunch of grapes on a windblown hillside.

The tranquil village of St. Saphorin descends abruptly from its vineyards to the shores of the Lake of Geneva.

Attention to detail and a sense of order carry over into just about every aspect of life. Notice how the pedestrians wait interminably for the traffic light to change rather than dart across an empty street. Even in French-speaking (hence relatively more relaxed) Lausanne, the métro trains depart every seven and a half minutes—by the second-hand. This seems all the more remarkable when you consider that one out of every seven inhabitants is a foreigner: a political exile, a "guest worker" or a tax-sensitive film star.

From any café table or park bench you can observe a cross-section of Swiss society: old ladies in hats with overfed dogs, conservatively dressed businessmen, well-mannered children, neatly uniformed street-cleaners shining the pavements with mechanical scrubbers, less neatly uniformed citizen-soldiers. Militiamen lugging their automatic rifles off to an annual spell of training are a visible fact of life in peaceful, neutral Switzerland. The country bristles with permanent preparations against foreign attack: tank traps, camouflaged bunkers, airstrips hidden in bucolic valleys, and an army reserve comprising nearly every able-bodied male up to the age of 50. "Armed neutrality" is the official stance, and no potential aggressor could possibly miss the hint.

Standard two-dimensional maps of Switzerland don't convey the country's geographical realities, which are based much more on altitude than latitude or longitude. About two-thirds of the land is mountainous. Some peaks rise up to 15,000 feet. Among the

jagged "highlights" are the mystical Matterhorn on the Swiss-Italian border and the imposing trio of Eiger, Mönch and Jungfrau commanding the Bernese Oberland. To the east, the poetic mountainsides of the Grisons provide the setting for renowned resorts like Arosa, Davos and St. Moritz.

Between the Alps to the southeast and the green and rocky Jura chain to the north-west, Switzerland's fertile plateau arcs from Lake Geneva to Lake Constance. At once pastoral and industrialized, this narrow swath takes in all the sizable cities and most of the confederation's 6½ million inhabitants.

The German speaking majority occupies the greater part of the country, except for the west and south-east. The centre of gravity for Swiss-Germans is Zurich, the metropolis of Switzerland. In in-

13

ternational finance, Zurich means a cool judgement that can make or break a company or a country. But for the visitor the town offers a placid setting, elegant shopping, museums and music and a lively, colourful history.

Geneva, the major city in the French-speaking area, has a more cosmopolitan air because of its location on the frontier with France and its vocation as neutral host to dozens of international organizations. Like Zurich, Geneva enjoys a lake- and riverside situation, easy access to the ski slopes, and an uncommonly comfortable way of life.

About midway between the two linguistic capitals is the political capital of the confederation, Berne—clearly a compromise among the competing magnets. Don't bother looking for heroic monuments or grandiose boulevards: Berne is too Swiss for pomposity. But the site and architecture of the city make it one of Europe's most pleasant capitals.

All the cities and towns of Switzerland share a tidy allure, yet each is distinctive in its atmosphere and accent, traditions and interests. It's no more than a morning's drive from the covered bridges of Lucerne to the orange trees of Lugano in the heart of the Italian-speaking section, but the change of language, culture and climate is as dramatic as the Alps that separate them.

Switzerland's villages are also well worth exploring. Of more than passing interest are the traditional costumes (still worn in remoter parts) and crafts, the architecture (perhaps an ensemble of medieval houses), or the landscape itself. The village fountain, where the cows pause to drink, may be a venerable work of art.

Unless you've come to see museums and historic churches —with which the country is more than adequately endowed —you'll probably spend most of your time outdoors in the deliciously pure air. The choice of activities couldn't be larger. You can climb a mountain or ride a horse. Ski (the year round!) or play tennis or golf. Swim or sail, hang-glide, water-ski or fish. If all you want to do is take a walk in the woods, follow the yellow signs posted all over the countryside. The thoughtful Swiss actually tell you how many minutes (or hours) it will take to reach the end of the trail.

Shopping is exceptionally worthwhile in Switzerland. Show windows display a seductive range of luxury merchandise: watches, jewellery, the latest in clothing from Italy and France. If your budget keeps you outside looking in, you can still enjoy all the colour of a street market. Once or twice a week almost every town and village has an outdoor bazaar stocked with a seasonal

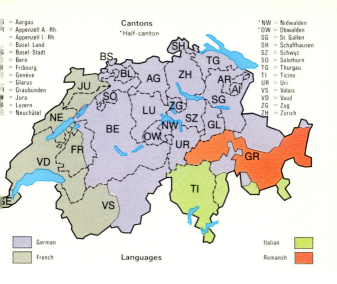

array of flowers, fruit and vegetables, home-made sausages and bread, and hand-crafted articles.

Eating out need not involve *haute cuisine*. The setting itself—high on a mountain, or alongside a lake—often takes priority. Local cooks strive to satisfy, offering up home-style food in almost overwhelmingly generous quantities. Switzerland's famous cheeses, of course, deserve special attention.

Nightlife is assuredly not a Swiss speciality. Yet even in Calvin's old town, Geneva, nightclub patrons revel far into the night; and Zurich has a genuine red-light district. By way of simpler pleasures, you can stop in at any café and try the wine from just up the hill. There's no hurry: the regulars spend hours over a carafe of wine or a cup of coffee, reading the newspapers, rolled onto sticks.

World travellers are accustomed to finding Swiss specialists running the best hotels in all the major cities and resorts. But not all these experts are abroad. Everywhere in Switzerland the hotels, whether grand or modest, hit high standards of comfort and cleanliness, the professionalism of the polyglot staff also makes a good impression. Even hospitality is efficient in this well-ordered world of scenic grandeur, the homeland of tourism.

FACTS AND FIGURES

Geography:	Area 15,940 square miles, about half the size of Ireland or twice that of New Jersey. Switzerland shares frontiers with West Germany, Austria, Liechtenstein, Italy and France. The highest point is Dufour Peak (Monte Rosa), 15,200 feet above sea level. The lowest point is Lake Maggiore, 635 feet above the sea. Most of the population inhabits the plateau between the Jura Mountains and the Alps.
Population:	Nearly 6½ million. About one resident in seven is a foreigner.
Major Cities:	Zurich (365,000), Basle (180,000), Geneva (155,000), Berne (145,000), Lausanne (125,000).
Government:	Multi-party, decentralized democracy. Confederation of 23 cantons (three of which are divided into six half cantons). Executive power held by a seven-member Federal Council. Bicameral legislature (Council of States with members from each canton and half canton and directly elected National Council). The two houses in turn elect the Federal Council and president.
Economy:	Highly developed and notably prosperous. Main exports: precision instruments, watches, machinery, chemicals, pharmaceuticals, electronics, textiles. There is one banking office for every 1,333 inhabitants.
Religion:	Catholic (47%), Protestant (44%).
Languages:	The four national languages are German (spoken by 75% of the population), French (20%), Italian (4%), Romansh (1%). English is spoken widely in tourist and business circles.

16

HISTORY

Thousands of years before William Tell, glaciers covered Switzerland. The first known inhabitants were cave dwellers who survived by hunting and gathering berries. When the glaciers retreated some 5,000 years ago, the people settled near the lakes and rivers left by the melting ice; they lived in huts on platforms supported by stakes.

Around 400 B.C. a Celtic people, the Helvetians, arrived. From them derives the original name of Switzerland, Helvetia. In 58 B.C. the Helvetians, seeking new territory, dramatically burned their farms and settlements and moved south-west; an estimated 370,000 were on the march, only to be stopped by the Roman legionaries of Julius Caesar who then followed them back and colonized the region. The Romans set up their administrative centre at Aventicum—now the sleepy town of Avenches between Lausanne and Berne.

They built roads through Helvetia, bringing their technology and culture, and, eventually, the new religion of Christianity. But with the collapse of the Roman empire, the eastern half of the country fell largely to the Alemanni, fierce Germanic tribesmen, while the west came under the control of the Burgundians. The dividing line between the two zones of influence, the River Sarine, more or less defines—to this day—the linguistic and cultural frontier between German-speaking and French-speaking Switzerland.

The Middle Ages

Soon both Alemanni and Burgundians were subdued by the Franks, one of the most powerful of the Germanic tribes. Under Charlemagne (768–814), the whole of what we know as Switzerland was incorporated into the Holy Roman Empire. Great abbeys were built, which later became centres of learning and culture.

With the demise of the Carolingian dynasty (911) began centuries of intrigue and politicking between the powerful medieval families—Zähringen, Kyburg, Habsburg. By the middle of the 13th century, two powers predominated: the House of Savoy and the Habsburgs. In central Switzerland resistance to widening Habsburg influence led to a mutual assistance pact linking three valley communities—Uri, Schwyz and Unterwalden (The name "Switzerland" is derived from the name of the founding canton of Schwyz.) The date, August 1, 1291, is commemorated as a national holiday.

During the next century the alliance developed into a confederation of eight cantons united against foreign aggression. This was the era of William Tell, who shot an apple from the head of his small son at 100 paces. Actually, discrepancies in the story of Tell, foe of tyrannical overlords, have led most historians to conclude that Switzerland's greatest hero lived in legend only. Or, as others put it, there has been no historical confirmation.

Nobody, however, can doubt the courage and prowess of the Swiss soldier of the time. In the Burgundian wars (1474–77) the confederation fought with ferocity against Charles the Bold, winning battle after battle—Grandson and Murten in 1476, Nancy in 1477.

Memories of medieval wars: Charles the Bold in flight, Chillon Castle.

Turn of the Tide

As a European military power, Switzerland was undefeated until 1515, when the army was overwhelmed by the vastly superior numbers of French troops in the Battle of Marignano (northern Italy). The French soldiers killed over 12,000 people.

The following year, a treaty of perpetual peace with France was signed by the confederation, which now counted 13 cantons. This marked the end of Swiss power politics and the beginning of neutrality — a stance that became as enduringly Swiss as the mountains. Swiss troops hired themselves out to foreign armies as mercenaries. The sight of these tough peasants with their heavy, deadly halberds had a devastating effect on enemy morale. Descendants of the halberdiers, in medie-

The Tell Affair

In a country without kings, history is made by common folk. Switzerland's national hero, William Tell, was a simple but cheeky farmer who stood up to the wicked governor.

Early in the 14th century Tell, visiting the town of Altdorf with his young son, refused to salute the governor's hat, which served as a symbol of Habsburg authority. The governor, the evil Gessler, arrested him and ordered him to shoot an apple from his son's head.

Tell scored a bullseye. However, Gessler noticed he'd taken two arrows from his quiver. When asked why, Tell admitted that if he had missed, the second arrow would have been for Gessler.

The infuriated governor ordered him imprisoned. But during the boat trip to the castle dungeon, a great storm tormented Lake Lucerne. William Tell was the only person able to steer the boat. He brought it safely to shore at a place now called Tellsplatte and managed to escape. Later, lying in wait in a grove near Küssnacht, he slew the tyrant.

Friedrich Schiller's play about the incident packs the open-air theatres of Interlaken and Altdorf every summer. Although most historians consider the story apocryphal, few people fret about the factual authenticity.

val finery as of old, may still be seen on guard at the Vatican... the only Swiss warriors in foreign service today.

During the 16th century chronic tensions within Europe were drastically heightened by the Protestant Reformation. In 1522, five years after Martin Luther hammered home his 95 theses in Germany, a Swiss curate, Ulrich Zwingli of Zurich, challenged the pope's authority. Over the next few years the cantons of Zurich, Berne and Basle sided with the forces of Reformation. The Bernese occupied the canton of Vaud and brought the Reformation with them. By 1541 the French reformer John Calvin had established a strict Protestant theocracy in Geneva, and his influence spread. As the Reformation and Counter-Reformation surged through Switzerland, blood was spilled on both sides.

But the Swiss were able to stay clear of Europe's great religious and political struggle, the Thirty Years' War (1616–48). The cantons joined forces to create a federal army, and Swiss Catholics and Protestants tried to live together peacefully behind the shield of armed neutrality. Meanwhile they prospered by supply-

The Swiss mountains have echoed to the mellow tone of alphorns since the time of the Romans.

The vegetable market takes over a patrician square in Solothurn.

ing both sides of the conflict. When peace finally came to Europe in 1648 with the Treaty of Westphalia, the independence of the sovereign state of Switzerland was at last universally acknowledged. Berne was the dominant canton.

The after-shock of the French Revolution (1789) reverberated throughout Europe, not least in Switzerland. After occupying or annexing attractive slices of Swiss territory, the French imposed the so-called Helvetic Republic. Most Swiss abhorred its artificial, centralized structure.

After three years of anarchy, Napoleon Bonaparte gave Switzerland a new constitution based on the old confederation, as well as six new cantons, bringing the number up to 19. He also took Swiss conscripts with him to foreign fields: 8,000 Swiss died covering the emperor's retreat from Moscow. Then, as the empire disintegrated, Russians, Austrians and Prussians occupied Swiss territory.

Neutral but Caring

With the Congress of Vienna (1815) Switzerland's "perpetual neutrality" was restored. Three more western cantons joined the confederation, establishing the present boundaries of the country. But religious strife between Catholics and Protestants returned to plague Switzerland. In 1846 the Catholic cantons separated from the confederation and fighting broke out, but the federal army quickly restored the peace. Political stability and national unity were fostered by a new constitution, proclaimed in 1848, which established Switzerland's grass-roots democratic institutions, with power shared by local, cantonal and federal authorities. Revised by the constitution of 1874, the set-up remains in force.

Swiss neutrality faced two harrowing tests in the 20th century —the world wars. In each case both army and people were mobilized to defend the confederation at any cost. In the summer of 1940 invasion by Hitler seemed a very real possibility. Switzerland's commanding general, Henri Guisan, is considered a great national hero—not for winning the war but for forging an army impressive enough to keep the country out of it.

Neutrality has conferred on Switzerland a position unique in world affairs—and far more importance than its size or even economic power would otherwise merit. Switzerland's special role began in 1863 when a businessman from Geneva, Henri Dunant, founded the Red Cross. (Its symbol, a red cross on a white background, is the reverse image of the Swiss flag.) The country has given asylum to political exiles of nearly all persuasions, from Lenin to Solzhenitsyn. The League of Nations was born in Geneva, later to become European headquarters of the United Nations. But Switzerland has held back from joining the U.N. itself, for fear of prejudicing national neutrality (though Switzerland does belong to numerous international organizations).

Today, this small country stands as a model of democracy, stability and prosperity for much of the world. The Swiss now face the challenge of striking a balance between commercial interests and moral considerations, between disengagement and humanitarian principles, trying to preserve their unique assets while finding their role in a changing world.

THE ESSENTIALS

If you're visiting Switzerland for the first time, you'll want to concentrate on the genuine highlights. Summarizing some of the sightseeing "musts", we propose the following list of short tours.

Inevitably there is an arbitrary and subjective element in our choices, but they may help you decide between alternatives. Travel agents in the major towns and tourist centres organize a variety of excursions by bus lasting one day or longer.

Zurich and Lucerne:
Zurich riverside, old town and museums
Lucerne riverside, museums
Lake Lucerne boat trip
Rigi
Mt. Pilatus
(2–3 days)

North-east Switzerland:
Schaffhausen
Rhine Falls
Stein am Rhein
St. Gall
Appenzell countryside
(3 days)

The Grisons:
Chur
Davos
Klosters
Engadine resorts
Zernez (National Park)
(4–5 days)

Ticino:
Locarno
Lake Maggiore
Ascona
Lugano and lake
(3 days)

Berne and Bernese Oberland:
Berne old town, bear pit, museums
Thun and lake
Interlaken
Grindelwald and Jungfraujoch
Gstaad
(3–4 days)

The Valais:
St-Maurice
Sion
Zermatt and Matterhorn
Saas-Fee
(3 days)

Western Switzerland:
Geneva and lake
Lausanne
Montreux
Château de Chillon
Gruyères
Fribourg
(2–3 days)

Jura and north-west:
Neuchâtel and lake
Porrentruy
Franches-Montagnes
Basle old town, museums
(3 days)

WHERE TO GO

How you organize your trip will depend on several variables: where you are coming from and how you are travelling, the season, and, of course, your interests—mountains and lakes, historic sights, picturesque villages, sports, art.

Getting around Switzerland couldn't be easier. The highway system is highly developed, trains run precisely to timetable and almost every town has an efficient array of buses, trams, taxis, funiculars or whatever is appropriate to the terrain.

The survey that follows divides the country into a dozen regions, which correspond almost entirely to those established by the national tourist authority for its

area offices. In a country as small as Switzerland, it's no problem to visit more than one district in a day. However, we don't recommend seeing Switzerland in a rush. There's a great deal to discover off the beaten path. Nearly every town and village has something to offer, it seems.

We begin with Zurich, the biggest Swiss city, served by the country's busiest international airport. After covering the pastoral north-east, bordering Germany, we venture across the undefended border to Liechtenstein. Safely back in Switzerland, we go north-west to Basle, an industrial but appealing city. The federal capital, Berne, leads to the popular tourist area around Interlaken. From there we turn to the historic central area with Lucerne its capital. Then eastwards to the charming Grisons and on to Italian-speaking Ticino. Continuing clockwise around Switzerland, we consider the rugged mountain country of the Valais. Then the French-speaking western part of the country: the lake and mountain resorts of Vaud; the hills of the Jura. We end our survey in the international city of Geneva, another important gateway to Switzerland.

The order in which the regions are introduced in this book, it should be emphasized, bears no relation to their importance or desirability as tourist centres.

ZURICH

There's much more to Zurich (*Zürich*) than mere gold ingots and bank vaults. The lake and the river are liquid assets that add greatly to the appeal of the city and the general welfare of its inhabitants. The preserved area of guildhalls and medieval houses has great charm. And the modern shopping district glitters as few others can afford to.

Zurich's economic importance —financiers usually put it on a par with New York, London and Paris—may conjure up the idea of an impersonal metropolis. Yet with less than 400,000 inhabitants, the city is manageably sized and easy enough to explore. The "gnomes of Zurich" who wheel and deal in billions of francs' worth of foreign currencies may maintain a hectic pace, but the rest of the citizens are more relaxed. In spite of the Zurichers' reputation as humourless puritans, local people do find the time to enjoy the theatres and museums, restaurants and nightclubs, the water sports at the door and the mountains just up the road.

The status of Zurich as a financial capital is little more than a century old: the local stock exchange was founded in 1877. But the city's history goes back about as far as you care to look. In the Neolithic era settlers built stilthouse villages along the shores of the Lake of Zurich. Two thousand years ago the Romans established a customs post on a hill overlooking the River Limmat, the Lindenhof, now the city's geographical centre. It took another thousand years before Zurich was recognized as a town, soon to become a prosperous centre of silk-, wool- and linen-weaving industries. In 1351 Zurich joined the Swiss confederation. The noblemen and merchants had then recently agreed to share power with representatives of the tradesmen's guilds; the guildhalls are still among the most precious landmarks in the old town.

In the 16th century the priest Ulrich Zwingli brought the Reformation to Zurich, adding intellectual renown to the city's growing importance in business and politics. Down through the centuries Zurich has attracted scores of great men, from Goethe and Richard Wagner to Thomas Mann and Albert Einstein, James Joyce and V. I. Lenin. (Lenin and his Bolshevik colleagues left Zurich in 1917 aboard the famous "sealed train" that travelled across Germany to chaotic Petrograd—now Leningrad.) Also during World War I, the nihilistic art movement known as Dada was born in what was then Zurich's Café Voltaire.

Today art of all kinds is on show in the city's 50-plus galleries. And the University of Zurich, Switzerland's largest, and the Federal Polytechnic, considered one of the world's best engineering schools, set the intellectual tone.

Discovering Zurich

The **Bahnhofstrasse** (Railway Station Street), the most elegant shopping street in Switzerland, starts at the station and proceeds to the lake shore. Jewellery and watches, furs and fashions, antiques and objects of art—the shop windows disclose a world of luxury. Much of the street is barred to automobile traffic, making window-shopping even more pleasurable. For James Joyce this street symbolized the character of the city: "Zurich is so clean that you could spill minestrone on the Bahnhofstrasse and eat it up with a spoon."

The tree-shaded Bahnhofstrasse emerges onto Bürkliplatz at the waterfront. From the nearby bridge, Quaibrücke, you can admire a superb view of the lake.

The venerable **Fraumünster** dominates the west bank of the river. There has been a church here since 853, the year a convent was founded on the site. The present building dates back to the 13th century. Its lovely Romanesque choir has a surprise in store—modern stained-glass windows by Marc Chagall, completed in 1970 when the artist was 83 years old.

Zurich's finest Baroque building, the neighbouring **Zunfthaus zur Meise,** was constructed for the wine merchants' guild in 1757. Now it contains the ceramic collection of the Swiss National Museum; the guildhall also provides a favourite setting for fashion shows and fashionable weddings.

In the Münsterhof, the square behind the Zunfthaus zur Meise, stands another guildhouse, **Zunfthaus zur Waag.** Headquarters of the linen weavers' and hatmakers' guild from 1637, the building has been turned into a restaurant, as have many of Zurich's old guildhalls.

Narrow old-world streets lined

A riverside café in Zurich affords a view of Zwingli's cathedral.

with antique shops and boutiques lead to **St. Peterskirche.** Set in the 13th-century tower is a huge clock face, one of the largest in Europe, measuring nearly 30 feet in diameter. The Baroque hall, a confection of pink-orange marble pillars, delicate stuccowork and crystal chandeliers, dates from reconstruction of the church in the 18th century.

Picturesque streets lie all around: you may want to wander the winding **Augustinergasse,** leading back to Bahnhofstrasse, or the **Schipfe,** down by the riverside, Zurich's oldest lane.

If you climb the steep steps to the historic **Lindenhof,** you'll enjoy a good view of the Limmat with its flat-roofed river boats. The fountain in this shady square commemorates the women of Zurich, who saved the city from the Habsburgs in 1292. Their ploy was to parade in full battledress, convincing the encircling enemy that Zurich was crowded with defending troops.

Across the river, just opposite the Fraumünster, stands the cathedral, the **Grossmünster,** built between 1100 and 1250 on the site of a 9th-century church. This is the "mother church of the Reformation in German-speaking Switzerland"; Zwingli preached here from 1519 until his death on the battlefield in 1531. The cathedral's twin 15th-century towers, capped by 18th-century domes, make it the city's most distinctive landmark. Modern stained-glass windows by Augusto Giacometti light up the stark interior.

More Giacometti windows adorn the **Wasserkirche,** but the most spectacular feature of this late Gothic church is its riverside situation. Built right on the Limmat, the church once stood on an island where the patron saints of Zurich — Felix and Regula —

were said to have been beheaded by the pagan Roman governor.

On the east bank of the river are the historic guildhalls, each one more splendid than the next. Among the most outstanding: **Zunfthaus zum Rüden,** one-time gathering place of the nobility; **Zunfthaus zur Zimmerleuten,** the old carpenters' guildhall of 1708, graced with attractive oriel windows; and **Zunfthaus zur Saffran,** headquarters of the haberdashers' guild. Opposite the latter is the **Rathaus,** the richly ornamented town hall, completed in 1698. Zurich's city and cantonal parliaments still meet here. The entire old town area invites carefree wandering: stroll along **Neu-**

markt, one of the best preserved of old Zurich streets, and on to the interesting high Gothic **Predigerkirche** in Zähringerplatz. Beyond lies Niederdorf, Zurich's red-light district. The bars, restaurants and attractions here comprise the city's hottest nightlife centre.

Zurich's Museums

East of the old town at Heimplatz, the **Kunsthaus** (Fine Arts Museum) surveys European painting (mainly German and French) from the Middle Ages to the 20th century. Particularly well represented are Swiss artists such as Johann Heinrich Füssli (who

tion. Room after room exhibits medieval religious sculpture, paintings, stained-glass windows and murals detached from ancient churches and houses. Upstairs, a cathedral-sized hall features historic weapons, armour, uniforms and battle standards. Rooms from Swiss houses several centuries old have been transplanted intact.

One more institution demands mention: the **Rietberg Museum** (Gablerstrasse 15), set in a lush park of exotic trees — fittingly enough: for the subject here is the art of Asia, Africa and America. Baron von der Heydt collected the pieces on display: traditional Chinese scroll paintings, Armenian carpets, Indian statuary, Peruvian pottery, African masks and more.

By Land, River and Lake

An offbeat tour of the city centre is conducted aboard the *Goldtimer*, a renovated trolley-car of 1920s vintage. This appealing one-hour circuit begins in the Bahnhofstrasse — but only between May and the middle of October.

A veteran funicular, the Polybahn, runs from the top of Seilergraben up to the panoramic terrace of the Federal Polytechnic.

changed his name to John Fuseli when he settled in England in the 1760s), Arnold Böcklin and Ferdinand Hodler, major figures of the 19th century, and the expressionist sculptor Alberto Giacometti. In addition to masterpieces by Monet, Cézanne, Van Gogh and Picasso, the museum has the biggest Edvard Munch collection outside Scandinavia. Works by Chagall fill an entire gallery; another is given over to Dada and its leading proponents, Hans Arp, Francis Picabia and Max Ernst.

Swiss culture, art and history are on display at the **Schweizerisches Landesmuseum** (Swiss National Museum), a vast Victorian structure behind the railway sta-

Departures are every three minutes.

For an excellent overall **panorama** of Zurich, its lake and the Alps, take the train from Selnau station—15 minutes by foot from Paradeplatz in the city centre—to Üetliberg, altitude

Zurich's guilds usher in springtime with formality and fresh flowers.

2,858 feet. The ride takes 25 minutes and trains leave every half hour.

Or view the city from the perspective of the river. Between April and October glass-topped boats leave every half hour from the Landesmuseum; the tour lasts 50 minutes. You float past the old town houses, guildhalls and churches, out into the lake and on to Zürichhorn park. On the way

back the boat stops at Enge, near the Rietberg Museum.

Zurich's lake, the **Zürichsee,** extends 25 miles from the end of the Bahnhofstrasse to Schmerikon, on the Obersee, and it reaches oceanworthy depths. A good way to see the lake is by excursion boat. You can take a quick lunchtime trip or short (1½ hour) and long (4- to 5-hour) cruises—travelling past quaint villages, extensive orchards and vineyards, and attractive little inns. The lakeside villages, especially those on the right bank, make up Zurich's wealthiest suburbs, known as the "Gold Coast".

Winterthur

It's a short hop to Winterthur—just 15 minutes on the expressway that leads beyond Zurich's airport. The small industrial city contains a laudable complement of greenery and artistic monuments. And the heart of old Winterthur preserves some admirable buildings from the 16th to the 18th centuries.

Winterthur probably has more works of art per inhabitant than any other town in Switzerland. The city owes its artistic eminence to local industrialists like Oskar Reinhart, who took time out from his vast business empire to indulge a private passion for collecting works of art. When Rein-

hart died in 1965 at the age of 80, he bequeathed his hoard of masterpieces to the nation.

Half the collection is on view in a massive 19th-century building right in the centre of town, the **Oskar Reinhart Foundation** (Stadthausstrasse 6). Here you'll see some 500 choice works by Swiss, German and Austrian artists of the 18th, 19th and 20th centuries. Take special notice of the German master, Caspar David Friedrich. And don't overlook the room full of portraits, landscapes and narrative paintings by Ferdinand Hodler, or the memorable children's portraits by his contemporary, Albert Anker.

The rest of the collection is housed in **Am Romerholz,** the steep-roofed suburban villa where the benefactor used to live. Any city of five million inhabitants would be proud to have the old masters and French Impressionists Reinhart amassed, from the elder Cranach and Brueghel to Cézanne and Van Gogh. A single hall is inadequate for all the Daumier drawings, watercolours and oils.

Industry wins out over art at Oberwinterthur, north-east of town. Here a museum called **Technorama** deals with aspects of technology from home appliances to industrial and engineering achievements; exhibits range from primitive engines to the latest computer equipment.

33

NORTH-EAST SWITZERLAND

Busy with commerce and industry, north-east Switzerland borders the international lake called Bodensee, better known abroad as Lake Constance. There are pleasant farms and vineyards and towns throughout this peaceful corner of the land, and the countryside is green and gently rolling.

You Can Bank on It

Many a novelist and film scenarist has cashed in on Swiss banks—the dramatic possibilities of their air of sophistication, discretion and mystery. Even the cool efficiency is impressive. In what other country could you walk into almost any bank in almost any town and cash your baht, cruzeiros *or* dinar *without creating a problem, a sensation or an all-out crisis?*

The most glamorous aspect of a Swiss bank, for the thriller writer, is the numbered account. But all accounts, by number or name, are locked in secrecy under a law enacted in 1934, designed to foil Hitler's attempts to track down the assets of German Jews. Whatever the original motives, the officially decreed silence of Swiss bankers opened the floodgates to billions of francs' worth of currency in flight, sometimes from disreputable sources. Swiss caution provides a haven for the assets of tax evaders, extortionate dictators and underworld overlords. But it also protects the smallest, most law-abiding bank client. And the success of Swiss banks gives the country's economy in general a rousing international vote of confidence.

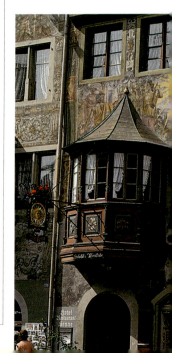

Schaffhausen

An industrial and communications centre on the River Rhine, **Schaffhausen** is the capital of Switzerland's northernmost canton, which juts out into Germany like the superfluous piece of a jigsaw puzzle. The old town centre of Schaffhausen, now a delightful pedestrian zone, counts as one of Switzerland's most magnificent.

Houses of the 16th to 18th centuries are embellished with statues, reliefs, elaborate allegorical frescoes and richly carved oriels (windows that project from the upper storeys—a feature of buildings throughout the northeast). In about 1570 Tobias Stimmer painted Haus zum Ritter in

Painted façades in Stein am Rhein.

Vordergasse with scenes from mythology and Roman history. Of the houses around the square in **Fronwagplatz,** notice especially the imposing **Grosses Haus,** which combines Gothic, Baroque and Rococo elements. The Renaissance-era **Haus zum Goldenen Ochsen** in Vorstadt stands out for the perfection of its carved decoration, depicting the five senses.

The 12th-century monastery of **Allerheiligen** (All Saints), just south, now contains a historical and fine arts museum rich in illuminated manuscripts and incunabula; alongside is a Romanesque abbey church *(Münster)* with a wooden ceiling. The monastery complex, since restored, was one of the historic sites badly damaged in 1944 when American war planes bombed Schaffhausen by tragic mistake.

Deer graze in the former moat surrounding the **Munot,** a vast circular fortress overlooking the town. You can reach the roof by climbing a spiral ramp inside the 16th-century keep. From the rooftop observation deck you look down on steeply sloped vineyards which produce a light and fragrant red wine, and on the town beyond and the Rhine that flows through it.

If you follow the river for a few kilometres on its way out of Schaffhausen, you'll come to Europe's biggest waterfall, the **Rheinfall.** (Several buses link town and falls.) Compared to Victoria Falls or Niagara, the Rhine Falls may seem a drop in the bucket. But with a flow that can reach about 38,000 cubic feet per second, it's as noisy as it is impressive. At this early stage in its journey the Rhine looks as clear and unpolluted as a mountain brook. The Rhine may be crossed by a high footbridge upstream from the falls (the right bank offers the most spectacular views). You can also take a boat to the midstream promontory to experience the thunder and rage of the falls.

Stein am Rhein (19 km. east of Schaffhausen) is a beautiful little town on the right bank of the river. In spite of the cars that clog these medieval streets, the place has tremendous appeal. All round the **market square** and adjacent main street are frescoed, half-timbered houses with stepped gables and oriels. Some of the buildings are over 400 years old. Often the decoration illustrates the name of the house—the White Eagle, the Inn of the Sun, the House of the Red Ox, and so on. The most repeated theme is that of St. George slaying the dragon, a motif contained in the municipal coat-of-arms. Local legend claims that the celebrated dragon was actually terrorizing the population near Stein am Rhein until the intrepid saint came to the rescue.

Kloster St. Georgen (St. George's Monastery) across from the town hall, founded by the Benedictines in the 11th century, has become a museum of local art and history. You can visit the rooms of the abbots of old, with their carved ceilings and *grisaille* (monochrome frescowork) decoration.

St. Gall

The textile centre of **St. Gall** (*St. Gallen* in German) lies 85 kilometres from Zurich, between Lake Constance and the pre-Alps of north-eastern Switzerland. Historic past and robust present come together in this dynamic town, Switzerland's seventh largest with a population of 75,000. Low-rise modern office buildings alternate with splendid houses of the 16th to 18th centuries. The likeable jumble is all reflected in the tinted windows of the new town hall, a mini-skyscraper next to the railway station.

The name, and very existence, of St. Gall can be traced back to a monk from Ireland, Gallus, who settled on the site in the early 7th century. About a hundred years later, a monastery was built in his memory, and soon an ecclesiastical town surrounded the abbey with houses and workshops, a school and a library. Manuscript illumination, poetry and music were practiced here by learned monks who made St. Gall a lead-ing centre of Germanic culture.

In the heart of the old town, extensive monastery buildings surround the **cathedral** (*Kathedrale* or *Stiftskirche*), one of the last great Baroque churches to be built in Europe (in the 1760s). Tall towers soar elegantly above the east façade. The exterior is relatively unadorned, but there is an impressive white and gold extravagance within.

The work of the dedicated monks of a thousand years ago can still be seen in the beautiful **Abbey Library** (*Stiftsbibliothek*), which occupies the west wing of the monastery complex. As you enter, you'll notice a Greek inscription over the door. It calls the library "The Medicine Chest of the Soul", and any book lover will agree with that description. In this Baroque treasure house the two-storey bookcases reaching to the frescoes on the ceiling hold 100,000 volumes. The collection of ancient manuscripts and incunabula alone (one of the world's richest) numbers 3,600. On display in glass cabinets are manuscripts of the 9th to 16th centuries—the most valuable are in Irish, Carolingian and Ottonian illuminated style.

The winding streets around the cathedral, some reserved for pedestrians only, contain a profusion of 16th- to 18th-century **houses.** The decorative elements include oriels, intricately carved

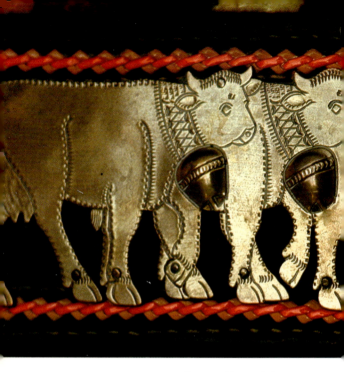

and painted, turrets, frescoes and ironwork. If you're in a rush, keep to Gallusstrasse, Schmiedgasse and Spisergasse.

St. Gall became a Free Imperial City in the year 1212. It soon gained fame as a producer of linen, and then cotton goods. Before World War I the area supplied two-thirds of the world's embroidered textiles. The technology and the products have changed, but St. Gall retains its reputation as textile capital of Switzerland. For a close look at some exquisite old fabrics visit the Industrie- und Gewerbemuseum in Vadianstrasse, which displays the Iklé and Jacoby collection of European lace, embroidery and tapestries.

Appenzell

It's just a short drive (30 km.) from St. Gall to Appenzell but once there you're worlds away from the comparatively sophisticated cathedral town. Appenzell lies in a small canton of the same name with an area of 160 square miles. Like an island, it's surrounded by the much larger canton of St. Gall.

Appenzell is a pastoral paradise: hilly grasslands, woods and high meadows lead up to low Alpine mountains. The countryside is strewn with pretty wooden houses while cows meander undisturbed outdoors. Hermann Hesse described the scene as "Sunday country".

The best time to be in the area is when the farmers drive the cows up to the high Alpine pastures *(Alpaufzug)* at the end of June or beginning of July, or when they bring them back in August or September. This is a festive event: men in traditional red waistcoats, yellow breeches and flower-trimmed hats carry milking stools decorated with rustic paintings, while the cows wear outsized, multi-coloured bells. What with the clanging, the mooing and an occasional outburst of yodelling, the procession happily disrupts life along the line of march.

A rich farm smell pervades the centre of **Appenzell**, where narrow streets are clogged with tourist traffic, tractors and motorbikes. Many of the houses are constructed of wood and adorned with brightly painted designs. The numerous souvenir shops here sell Appenzell's highly regarded hand embroidery, wooden buckets, cow bells, cheese and naïve paintings by local farmer-artists.

In a town as small as Appenzell you can scarcely miss **Landsgemeindeplatz**, an attractive square with plenty of space for outdoor cafés and restaurants. This is where a classic exercise in Swiss self-government occurs every year on the last Sunday of April. All the eligible men over 20 gather in the square, traditionally armed with ceremonial sword or dagger, to vote by show of hands for local officials and proposed laws. Since the dawn of democracy here, women have not shared the full franchise. They can vote on communal and federal but not on cantonal issues. Whatever your views on this controversial subject, it's best to avoid an argument with an Appenzeller about it.

Delightful pastoral panoramas unfold throughout the Appenzell district, and the villages are a repository of folklore and folk arts. Among names on the signposts: Gais, with a row of grand, gabled houses from the late 18th century on the main square; Trogen, a picturesque little town with its own *Landsgemeinde,* held every other year; Urnäsch, home of a regional museum full of furniture, costumes and jewellery; and Herisau, even bigger than Appenzell itself, with another museum devoted to local history and handicrafts.

The highpoint of the district is the **Säntis** (8,230 ft.). The roads to the mount end at Schwägalp, from which a year-round cable-car service approaches the summit. The view encompasses everything from the Bernina range in the Grisons Alps to Lake Constance.

From Schwägalp you can continue on to Neu St. Johann, gateway to the beautiful Upper Toggenburg region, and its chief resort, Wildhaus. Vaduz in Liechtenstein lies further along the road.

For men only: a show of hands at Trogen's age-old Landsgemeinde.

Foreign Intrigue: Liechtenstein

In a world of frontiers marked by barbed wire and bunkers, or at best a fringe of red tape, it's something of a novelty to cross the border from Switzerland to the Principality of Liechtenstein: no immigration officers, no customs men, no sentries impede your progress. Liechtenstein abolished its army more than a century ago, and nobody has bothered it since.

The area of this little country is about 60 square miles—a bit more than one-tenth the area of the city of Chicago. The status of the principality dates back to the beginning of the 18th century, when the German emperor declared its sovereignty under the aegis of the Prince of Liechtenstein. For much of the 19th century it formed part of the German confederation, then links to the bordering country of Austria were forged. The Swiss connection, established in 1923, is now so close that Liechtenstein's official currency is the Swiss franc.

The capital of **Vaduz** has a population approaching 5,000, including the ruling prince himself, whose castle stands high on the hillside. The castle, everything you'd expect of a medieval fortified residence, is not open to tourists. But the prince does display highlights from his superb collection of paintings in the **Liech-** **tensteinische Staatliche Kunst-sammlung** (National Art Gallery) in Städtle, the main street. Changing shows feature the works of the great Dutch and Flemish masters: Pieter Brueghel the Elder, Rubens, Van Dyck and Hals. The museum shares a building with the tourist information office and a small but definitive philatelic museum (Postmuseum).

In the same street, the **Landesmuseum** (National Museum) occupies a renovated building—originally an inn known as the Stag—which later served as the seat of government. Displays include locally excavated Stone Age relics and jewellery, Roman coins, weapons from the era of the Alemanni tribesmen (4th to 8th centuries, A.D.), and a folklore museum.

On the opposite side of the street, the modern post office looks rather large for the needs of a country of 26,000 people. But Liechtenstein, with its advantageous tax and banking laws, has attracted numerous foreign companies, represented by little more than a post office box.

Beyond Vaduz lie the forests, meadows and vineyards of Liechtenstein, producing seven principal wines as well as a local version of champagne. The villages, scattered through the hills and orchards, are noted for their charm.

NORTH-WEST SWITZERLAND

The zone the tourist authorities designate "north-west" (north-central might be more accurate) owes its history to its water resources. The conquerors who passed this way understood the strategic importance of the rivers of the region, starting with the mighty Rhine. And travellers since the time of the Romans have been attracted by the area's thermal baths.

Basle

The metropolis of north-west Switzerland, Basle *(Basel)* is the country's second biggest city (population 180,000) and principal port; from here Swiss exports travel the Rhine to the sea. With its skyline of smokestacks and construction cranes, Basle clearly is no ordinary Swiss town. But as industrial cities go, it has considerable charm, thanks to parks large and small, interesting architecture, an intense cultural life, and, always, the river itself.

Cosmopolitan Basle touches the frontiers of two foreign countries: Germany and France are just a handshake away. In one day you can visit the Black Forest, partake of the gastronomic delights of Alsace and, in transit, drop in on one of Basle's famous museums.

German Emperor Konrad II took the town over from Bur-gundy in 1033, and Basle remained German until 1501, when it entered the Swiss confederation as its eleventh member.

For centuries Basle has enjoyed an international reputation as a centre of learning and culture. A bishopric in the early 7th century, it went on to become the site of the first Swiss university, founded in 1460. When Desiderius Erasmus of Rotterdam came here to teach, the town developed into one of the greatest humanist centres north of the Alps.

Today Basle competes with Zurich for the title of Switzerland's wealthiest town. Three hundred years ago the burghers grew rich manufacturing silk; now the most important industries are chemicals and pharmaceuticals. Every year the Swiss Industries Fair attracts more than a million visitors to Basle. The city's active stock exchange is second in Switzerland to Zurich's. And the summit meetings of high finance take place here: once a month, the world's top central bankers convene in the 19-storey headquarters of the Bank for International Settlements. On that day even Zurich financiers keep a wary eye on the news from Basle.

Exploring the City

Don't let the distant smokestacks discourage you. Despite all the industry and commerce, Basle is a thoroughly enjoyable Swiss city

with a charming old town. A likely place to start is the Tourist Office, overlooking the Rhine at Blumenrain 2—for brochures, advice and reasonably priced guided tours.

Baslers let their hair down for the three-day fantasy of carnival.

From here it's a few steps to the **Mittlere Rheinbrücke,** one of the six bridges that span the river. From here you have a perfect **view** of the real Basle: upstream the cathedral surrounded by magnificent medieval houses; downstream the chemical works that fuel local prosperity.

You can also cross the river aboard a small ferryboat. A fare is charged, making this a very profitable enterprise, for the ecologically perfect system uses no fuel at all. The river's own power propels

Fasnacht

Carnival in Basle is famous throughout Europe, for Baslers have a reputation as great wits. The gaudy three-day revel, complete with fanciful masks, fifes and drums, extraordinary costumes and giant lanterns, starts in the wee hours of the Monday morning after Ash Wednesday. As processions ebb and flow through the narrow streets, politicians become fair game for satirists, the bars are crowded around the clock, and business takes second place, or surrenders completely.

the boat, attached to an overhead cable, across the stream.

Little Basle *(Kleinbasel)* on the far side of the Rhine offers a splendid **panorama** of Great Basle on the left bank, with its quirky old skyline. Stroll the agreeable riverside promenade, the **Oberer Rheinweg**, lined with attractive 18th and 19th century houses. At No. 93 look for the scale showing the Rhine flood levels since 1641, when river barges could have tied up at the front door.

Returning to the older and more aristocratic Great Basle, you can hardly miss the notorious Lällekeenig, an impertinent bit of sculpture on the building at Schifflände 1. The Lällekeenig, a medieval king's head with its tongue poking out, is the Great Basler's

way of showing scorn for his brothers across the Rhine. Little Basle's response can be witnessed every January on Vogel Gryff (griffon) day, when the Wilde Mann (savage) climbs onto the bridge from a raft, performs a contemptuous dance and finally shows the Lällekeenig his backside. Until well into the 20th century, "proper" people in Great Basle boycotted this ceremony—although some secretly watched through binoculars. Vogel Gryff day sets the tone for the riotous pre-carnival period.

It's an uphill climb from the river to Basle's most perfect square, the 18th-century **Münsterplatz,** once the site of a Roman fort. For the past thousand years or so a church has stood here. The present red sandstone **Münster** (cathedral) still looks much the way it did in the 12th century. With its twin barbed spires rising high above the Rhine, the cathedral was the seat of powerful bishop-princes who ruled the town for centuries, until the Reformation drove them out.

Admire the sculptural detail of the main Gothic entranceway. Then go round the side of the building to the **Galluspforte,** a fine Romanesque portal that was really intended as the cathedral's main entrance. Why it ended up on the transept, nobody knows; some wags have suggested it might simply have been a mis-

45

take. Inside, visitors always stop to read the epitaph of the scholar Erasmus, who died in Basle in 1536.

You should also take in the view from the **Pfalz,** the terrace behind the apse. The combination of the fast-flowing Rhine waters immediately below, the Little Basle waterfront and the hills of the Black Forest rising in the background is memorable.

Basle's big modern theatre, the **Stadttheater** in Theaterstrasse, stands on a multilevel plaza — site of a whimsical mechanical fountain by Jean Tinguely.

The main shopping streets — Freiestrasse, Falknerstrasse and Gerbergasse — lead through the centre of town to **Marktplatz,** a thriving marketplace for fruit, vegetables and flowers. Facing the square is one of Basle's most striking buildings, the 16th-century **Rathaus** (Town Hall). This symbol of civic pride boasts turrets, towers, arches, Renaissance windows and a glittering gold steeple.

A long, ambitious project to encircle Basle with a city wall was completed in 1398. Very little of the fortifications survived the urban development plans of the 19th century, but one impressive monument has been saved: **Spalentor,** western gateway to the city, surmounted by a clock tower and flanked by two crenellated watch towers. The sculptures portraying

Mary and the prophets (15th century) were added somewhat later.

On the south-west side of town, not far from the railway station, is Basle's **Zoologischer Garten** (known locally as the *Zolli*), the biggest zoo in Switzerland. Founded more than a century ago as a serious scientific institution, this is the first zoo in Europe where the gorilla, one-horned rhinoceros and other species have reproduced in captivity.

Basle's Museums

Few institutions can rival the holdings of the prestigious **Kunstmuseum,** nearby at St. Albangraben 16, the first art museum in Europe to open to the general public. It all began in 1662, when the town and the university bought the private art collection of a local law professor. Among the paintings were 15 portraits by Hans Holbein the Younger of his Basle contemporaries, including Erasmus. Old masters still hold their own here, but the museum has kept pace with the times, adding artists as modern as Rothko, Jasper Johns, Calder and Newman. Perhaps the most farsighted of recent acquisitions was the purchase of numerous late works by Picasso, a period

The Museum of Contemporary Art's levitation sensation is only a statue.

ignored by many other institutions. The constructions of Jean Tinguely, a mischievous Swiss sculptor, are among the most popular exhibits. Consult the directory in the foyer to find the numbers of the rooms you wish to visit. Among artists well represented: Konrad Witz, Martin Schongauer, Hans Baldung Grien, Dürer, Rembrandt, Basle's own Arnold Böcklin, Monet, Gauguin, Picasso, Braque and Chagall.

It takes just ten minutes to walk from the Kunstmuseum to Basle's riverside **Museum für Gegenwartskunst** (Museum of Contemporary Art) at St. Albantal 2. The collection is housed in an old paper mill transformed out of all recognition in 1980. There are big bay windows and a magnificent atrium—the perfect setting for Jonathan Borofsky's *Flying Man,* a sculpture that swoops down from the region of the third floor. Conceptual and minimal works by Frank Stella, Donald Judd, Carl André and Joseph Beuys contrast with the extravagant new expressionism of Mimmo Paladino, Enzo Cucchi and Francesco Clemente. You'll also see some Swiss exponents of the new representation. The museum chronicles recent developments—art as timely and controversial as tomorrow's headlines.

Another of the city's two dozen or more museums is situated in the St. Albangraben area: **Haus zum Kirschgarten** (Elisabethenstrasse 27), an 18th-century mansion filled with objects that evoke the comfortable world of the Basle burgher, like porcelain stoves and tableware, chandeliers and clocks. Each room is devoted to a different style: Baroque, Louis XVI and Restoration.

Excursions Around Basle

In just a quarter hour by car, you can reach any of these charming spots in the Basle countryside: **Arlesheim,** to the south, a village surrounded by woods, fields and cherry orchards, is the site of a Baroque collegiate church *(Domkirche)* with a graceful Rococo façade and interior. The fine houses on the church square were built for the canons of the chapter in the 18th century. On the skyline stand three medieval castles.

The neighbouring village of **Dornach** is dominated by the fascinating **Goetheanum,** a theatre designed in the 1920s in revolutionary form by the founder of the Anthroposophic movement, Rudolf Steiner. The expressionist architecture, which excludes all right angles, is not to everybody's taste, but somehow this extraordinary ferro-concrete block blends into the surrounding hills. Among other activities, Goethe's plays are often performed here, hence the name.

East of Basle, the motorway

goes past **Augst,** once known as Augusta Raurica and now sometimes referred to as "Switzerland's Pompeii". The 20,000-strong population of this flourishing Roman outpost (founded around 44 B.C.) enjoyed such facilities as a theatre, forum and thermal baths, the ruins of which are all visible. In the summer, you can watch a play in the well-preserved outdoor theatre or visit the museum of treasures unearthed on the site—the first Roman settlement on the Rhine.

Solothurn

In sight of the Jura chain, this small town on the River Aare, about 65 kilometres south of Basle, also has a Roman past. But Solothurn's charm derives mainly from its Baroque aura. In the 17th and 18th centuries, the ambassadors and envoys of Catholic France chose to live in patrician mansions here, for Solothurn kept the faith in the face of the Reformation.

The monumental Baroque **St. Ursenkathedrale** (Cathedral of St. Ursus) looks startlingly Italianate. In fact, the architects who designed the building, Gaetano Matteo Pisoni and his nephew, Paolo Antonio, came from the Ticino. Outstanding features of the subdued interior include a pink marble pulpit and the painted decoration in the chancel and at the crossing of the transept. The treasury contains precious reliquaries and the Hornbach Missal, an illuminated manuscript of the 10th century.

The 17th-century **Altes Zeughaus** (arsenal), a street away off the main thoroughfare (*Hauptgasse*), has a fine collection of weapons and uniforms from medieval to modern times. You'll also see a 400-year-old figure of a knight who spits if you lift his helmet. On your way down Hauptgasse you'll notice the Baroque **Jesuitenkirche** (Jesuit Church), completed towards the end of the 17th century. Frescoes and delicate stuccowork adorn the nave. From the vantage point of a café table on the market square you can admire the 12th-century **Zeitglockenturm** (Clock Tower). The elaborately decorated astronomical clock itself dates back more than 400 years. City fathers conduct municipal business in style in the grandiose **Rathaus** (Town Hall) in Rathausgasse, a Gothic tower with domed extensions and Mannerist embellishments.

Solothurn has many small squares, each with its own historic fountain. Notice the old houses with heavy overhanging roofs and dormer windows of a peculiar local design; on lower floors, the windows are often too close together for the shutters to open all the way, so they stand out at right

49

angles or, more prosaically, over-lap. Guarding the old town (a pedestrian zone) are a couple of medieval gates, the Bieltor and the Baseltor.

Beyond the fortifications, just north of the old town in Werkhofstrasse, lies the **Kunstmuseum,** worth visiting if only for a look at the masterful *Virgin of Solothurn* by Hans Holbein the Younger.

Baden

The River Limmat cuts through Baden, a town some 60 kilometres east of Basle (22 km. from Zurich). Swiftly flowing, mostly unencumbered by elaborate embankments and quays, the river is lined with drooping trees and houses that back onto the water. The town itself is simple and unspoiled: there are some attractive 16th- and 17th-century houses, the ruin of an ancient fortress, and working vineyards on the hillsides.

Baden, meaning "baths", has been a spa for 2,000 years, since the era when Romans called it Aquae Helveticae. The hot springs here are really hot; the mineral-rich water gushes forth at 117° F. Visitors can take the cure either in the hotels (some quite luxurious) or in the municipal spa. The water here is said to relieve symptoms of rheumatic, neurological, respiratory and cardiovascular diseases.

For the visitor with or without medical motives, Baden offers some relaxed sightseeing, starting with the view from any of the heights—from the park in front of the casino *(Kursaal),* or from the modern bridge high above the river. The **panorama** stretches from the roofs of the old town to the unspoiled charm of the river.

A **clock tower** *(Stadtturm)* built in late Gothic style dominates the old town. Linked to it is a crenellated wall that goes up the hillside to the fortress called Stein Castle, which has been in ruins since the early 18th century.

Baden's 15th-century **Town Hall** (Rathaus) contains the historic assembly hall *(Tagsatzungssaal)* where representatives of Switzerland's original 13 cantons met at regular intervals from 1424 to 1712.

If you follow the old streets down to the riverside you can walk across a 19th-century covered bridge to the medieval **Landvogteischloss** (Bailiff's Castle). The grimness of this 15th-century stone tower is offset by boxes of flowers in all the windows. Inside, a museum displays old arms and artefacts from the surrounding district of canton Aargau; the upper floors offer grand views of the town with its quaint houses painted unpredictable colours, and no two roofs exactly the same height.

BERNE AND VICINITY

The canton of Berne, second largest in area of all the Swiss states, stretches from the French border in the north-west to the heights of the alps in the south. Because of the diversity of the terrain, its towns and natural attractions, the tourist authorities tend to divide it in two: the federal capital and the northern part of the region as one unit, and Interlaken and the alpine resorts—the Bernese Oberland—as another. We begin in the rolling green countryside near the frontier between the German- and French-speaking zones, where the Swiss placed their capital in a gesture of compromise.

Berne

Foreign diplomats assigned to embassies in Berne (*Bern* in German), the seat of Switzerland's federal government, find the life unsophisticated and provincial. That's the way the Swiss like it; for the same reason they prefer politicians who don't rock the boat. Berne (population 145,000) may not abound in scintillating cocktail parties and international intrigue, but there's no denying that it's full of character.

Berne looks back on nearly 800 years of often tempestuous history. Tradition claims that the town was founded in 1191 by Duke Berchtold V of Zähringen as an impregnable bastion on the western edge of his domain. The city's strategic position is still striking: it stands on a high, rocky peninsula formed by a loop in the River Aare. After a fire in 1405, which almost completely destroyed the wooden houses, Berne was rebuilt in sandstone. Today, bedecked with flowers and flags, the town retains such a medieval appearance that the old duke himself wouldn't look out of place riding down one of the wide, arcaded streets.

Were he to do so, he would find the Zähringen bear portrayed everywhere: in statuary, on flags, and very much alive in the ever-popular Bear Pit. According to legend, at the time of the town's foundation the duke vowed he would name the place after the first animal caught in a hunt in the nearby woods. A bear (*Bär* in German) was first to fall.

In 1353, having fought the Habsburgs for its freedom and independence, Berne joined the Swiss confederation. The city grew in power and influence. Its westward expansion ultimately drew the French-speaking part of the country into the confederation (see p. 20). When the constitution of 1848 was drafted, Berne was chosen as the centre of the federal government.

Despite this honour, there is practically no political pomp and very little ceremony. The seven members of the Federal Council carry on like ordinary citizens;

51

you might see them walking to work. Every Tuesday and Saturday morning the square in front of the Parliament building becomes a marketplace where the local populace mills about sizing up the onions and tomatoes. It tends to put politics into a very Swiss perspective.

Berne's Old Town

One place you might not expect to find vestiges of old Berne is the city's railway station, among the most modern in Europe. But in the spacious underground passages between the platforms and the street you can see the remains of the Christoffelturm, part of the town defences, dating back 600 years. The stones were carefully preserved when the new station was constructed.

If you take the escalator to street level, you emerge at the start of **Spitalgasse,** a lively shopping street whose department stores take refuge behind elegant old façades. The solid-looking arcades are characteristic of Bernese architecture. Because Berne has more than five miles of arcades, it's an especially good place to spend a rainy day. Spitalgasse and Marktgasse further on are barred to private cars, but watch out for the trams and trolley-buses!

At the beginning of Spitalgasse stands what has been called the most important Protestant Baroque church in Switzerland: the austere **Heiliggeistkirche** (Holy Ghost Church), constructed in the 1720s. To view the interior, you'll have to arrive half an hour before a Sunday service, as otherwise it's closed to the public.

Berne is a city of **fountains,** almost all built in the 16th century. The central columns generally support colourfully painted allegorical figures. The first fountain you come to is the Pfeiferbrunnen (Bagpiper Fountain), probably the work of Hans Gieng, who designed many of these local landmarks. While the theme of most of the fountains is clear, the meaning of this one remains a mystery.

The **Käfigturm,** over 300 years old, served as a prison tower and lookout. Today this relic of Berne's defences contains the municipal information centre, where slide shows are given in various languages. To the left of the tower lies Waisenhausplatz. The building at the far end of the square, the 18th-century Waisenhaus (orphanage), now shelters the police headquarters. The modern fountain by Meret Oppenheim makes a controversial addition to the city scene. To the right of the Käfigturm is Bärenplatz and its

Geared up for battle, a sculpted bear guards Berne's famous clock tower.

cafés and open-air chess sets with outsized pieces. A good match always draws a crowd of onlookers and commentators.

Beyond the Käfigturm, in **Marktgasse** are two typical Berne fountains: one shows temperance in a flowing blue gown, mixing wine with water, and the other portrays a flagbearer. An ogre is the subject of the **Kindlifresserbrunnen,** the fountain in Kornhausplatz, the next square to the left. On a slender column the child-eater sits poised to bite off the head of one victim, while others wait in his sack. The renovated Kornhaus and theatre dignify the square.

Berne's famous **Zytgloggeturm**

*Berne's annual onion festival
celebrates the humble onion.*

(Clock Tower) is so unusual you ought to schedule your sightseeing around its timetable. You must arrive (at the side facing away from the railway station) at least five minutes before the striking of the hour. Find a good vantage point and ready your camera for a rollicking display of 16th-century Swiss clockwork: a jester wriggles to ring two bells above his head, processions of bears follow, a cock crows and flaps his wings, and so on.

Beyond the Zytglogge in the upper part of **Kramgasse** stands the Zähringerbrunnen (Zähringen Fountain)—a warrior bear in armour standing proudly with a tiny bear at its feet—dedicated to the city's founder. Albert Einstein and his family lived at Kramgasse 49 between 1902 and 1909, the period when the physicist began to elaborate his theory of relativity. (The apartment where Einstein worked is now a small museum.)

Twin staircases grace the **Rathaus,** Berne's Gothic town hall, to the left off Kramgasse in its own little square. Here the co lourful Vennerbrunnen (Flagbearer Fountain) shows a Bernese standard-bearer in full uniform.

But the city's finest fountain must be the **Gerechtigkeitsbrunnen** (Justice Fountain), in the street of the same name, the **Gerechtigkeitsgasse** (the prolongation of Kramgasse). The sculpture is an allegory of Justice, who holds a sword and a delicately balanced set of scales; at her feet are the pope, emperor, sultan and bailiff.

At the end of the street, you're faced with two tempting choices of route: straight across the bridge to the Bear Pit or down the Nydeggstalden to the oldest, although most recently reconstructed, part of town. (Even if you can't resist the bears, it will be worthwhile coming back here afterwards.) The **Nydeggkirche** (Nydegg Church) dates to the 14th century, although the interior was completely renovated in 1953. Note the fine bronze reliefs illustrating scenes from the life of Christ on the doors. The statue in the courtyard depicts, naturally enough, the Duke of Zähringen.

Continuing downwards, the street levels out at Läuferplatz. Directly in front of you is the Untertorbrücke, Berne's oldest bridge (1461–1489). On the left, the Läuferbrunnen (Messenger Fountain) honours a Bernese herald who had the audacity to reply to a French king's complaint that he didn't speak French, "Well, you can't speak German!".

Over the bridge and straight up, it's a stiff 10-minute climb to the **Rosengarten.** The reward is a spectacular **view** of the old town. But if you can't face the climb, turn right after the Untertorbrücke and walk up the gradient to the **Bärengraben** (Bear Pit).

BERNE AND VICINITY

Bears have been kept in the city since the 15th century—except for a sad era when French troops occupied Berne and confiscated the municipal mascots. There can be as many as 20 bears in the three pits, but you'll probably see fewer—the others are busy indoors. Some of the biggest crowds gather on Easter Sunday when, weather permitting, the bear cubs are let out with their mother for their first spring outing.

Return over the Nydeggbrücke and continue up **Junkerngasse** with its fine 18th-century patrician houses to Berne's late Gothic **Cathedral** (*Münster*). The structure took centuries to build. Started in 1421, the nave was completed more than 150 years later, and the tip of the filigreed steeple was added as recently as 1893. The largest of the cathedral's bells—the largest in Switzerland, as well—was cast in 1611 and weighs more than 10 tons. The cathedral's greatest work of art is Erhart Küng's terrifying vision of the **Last Judgement** (1490–1495) above the main entrance. The relief shows members of all classes— high church dignitaries included —howling in eternal damnation.

Nydegg church (left) and cathedral spires uplift Berne's cosy skyline.

The 15th-century **stained-glass windows** in the chancel are impressive (especially the *Dance of Death*) and the Renaissance **choir stalls** magnificent. Examine the figures carved on them, portraying monks, cherubs, knights, jesters, a dairymaid, a baker and the bears of Berne. For the energetic, 254 spiral steps lead to the second terrace of the tower, which affords a **panorama** of the whole town and the peaks of the Alps beyond. But for another interesting view over Berne, without the climb, step out onto the shady **Münsterplattform** (cathedral terrace) alongside the church.

Off to the right you'll see the iron-arched Kirchenfeldbrücke, a busy bridge for trams and cars. The "castle" behind the trees on the opposite bank is, in fact, the Berne Historical Museum (see p. 59). And below, past the rooftops of the riverside houses, you can contemplate the River Aare on its rushing rounds.

One more landmark of Berne lies near by: the **Bundeshaus** (Federal Parliament Building), a palatial 19th-century building with an overblown façade. There are free guided tours (the guides speak English) six times a day, except during parliamentary sessions and on holidays.

Berne's **Tierpark Dählhölzli** (Zoo), in the southern suburbs, advertises an unusual speciality: it shelters only European animals—no lions or tigers or elephants. But hundreds of species may be seen, notably mountain dwellers like the ibex, chamois and marmot, native to Switzerland.

For a brief out-of-town excursion leading to a magnificent vantage point overlooking both Berne and the Bernese Alps, go to the **Gurten** (altitude 2,815 feet). Every half hour a funicular runs from Wabern, just south of the city centre, to the summit, a ten-minute journey. Unless you have a special permit, the only cars allowed are tiny, battery-powered children's runabouts; the whole area is a haven of peace and tranquillity.

Berne's Museums

The **Kunstmuseum** (Fine Arts Museum), a five minute walk from the railway station at Hodlerstrasse 12, is famed for its extensive Paul Klee collection (over 2,500 works). The artist was born (1879) and bred in Berne. The Klees benefit from rehanging in a splendid new wing, completed in 1983. Natural daylight illuminates these and other masterpieces of 20th-century art by Picasso, Kandinsky, Kirchner, Miró, etc. You'll also see old masters from Fra Angelico to Delacroix in a new light, as well as Albert Anker, Ferdinand Hodler and his followers.

Mountain climbers, skiers and

other admirers of the Alps will be interested in the **Schweizerisches Alpines Museum** (Swiss Alpine Museum), Helvetiaplatz 4, which features topographical reliefs of the mountains, displays of historic climbing and skiing equipment, and items showing the alpine way of life.

The **Schweizerisches PTT-Museum** (Swiss Postal Museum), downstairs in the same building, has fascinating mementoes of all aspects of the post, telegraph and telephone service, from stagecoaches and Victorian switchboards to modern telex machines. Rare stamps, Swiss and foreign, may be seen in the basement philatelic collection.

The extraordinary, mock 16th-century building of the **Bernisches Historisches Museum** (Berne Historical Museum), Helvetiaplatz 5, is really less than a century old. The exhibits range from arts and crafts to weapons, porcelain figures and jewellery. The highlight is the booty taken from the Duke of Burgundy in the battle of Grandson (1476), including battle standards, manuscripts and precious tapestries.

The collections of the **Naturhistorisches Museum** (Natural History Museum) at Bernastrasse 15 (near the Historical Museum) figure among Europe's richest. Zoology, geology, mineralogy and palaeontology are well represented and well displayed.

Biel

Prehistory and modern industry meet in Biel (*Bienne* in French), a town of rivers, brooks, canals and the lake of the same name, 32 kilometres north-west of Berne. A concentration of watch factories makes Biel the "Watch Capital" of Switzerland.

And an intriguing linguistic situation sets the town apart. About two-thirds of the population speak Swiss-German, the rest French. Virtually everyone in town is completely bilingual of necessity, and you can hear some astonishing conversations that switch languages in mid-phrase.

The old town, with medieval houses carefully restored to look as old as they are, lures the visitor to stroll for a while—especially along the arcaded **Obergasse.** The 16th-century fountains, like those of Berne, catch the eye, their statues painted in the boldest of colours. Notice especially the Flagbearer Fountain *(Vennerbrunnen)* with its man-at-arms in the central square, the **Ring,** an impressive architectural ensemble.

Prehistory is a preoccupation in Biel because of the achievements of a local archaeologist, Colonel Friedrich Schwab (1803–1869). The site he excavated at La Tène (near the shore of Lake Neuchâtel) gave the name to a culture of the late Iron Age. Biel's museum was donated to the town by Schwab, after whom it was named. Many of the Iron Age and Roman relics on display were discovered by the colonel himself.

From Biel, it takes about an hour and a half to walk out to the **Taubenloch Gorges** *(Taubenloch-schlucht)* and back. A footpath

The red-and-white flag flies high over a land of rolling green hills.

leads to the site, an area of wild beauty known as the "Gateway to the Jura".

Excursion boats on the lake go to **St. Peter's Island** *(St. Peters-insel),* about a 50-minute trip, each way. This nature preserve is an island in name only, since a drainage project last century (which enabled the excavation of ancient lake dwellings on the south shore) lowered the water

level and transformed it into a peninsula. St. Peter's Island captivated that "Friend of Nature", Jean-Jacques Rousseau, on a visit here in 1765. The hotel room where he stayed, filled with memorabilia, is a place of pilgrimage nowadays. Otherwise the attractions haven't changed: flowered fields, grazing horses, a few vineyards and peaceful, quite penetrable forests.

Emmental

The Emmental region—famous for its cheese—stretches east and north-east of Berne. It's a summation of rural Switzerland, green and restful, and so neat and tidy they even plait the dung heaps!

You travel through rich agricultural country with hills topped by pine woods to the town of **Burgdorf** *(Berthoud)*, now devoted to textile manufacture. The restored 12th-century castle houses a little museum of local history. From Burgdorf a pretty road follows the valley of the River Emme (which is what Emmental means) to the big village of **Langnau** (30 km. from Berne) in the heart of the region, which claims a fine, fog-free climate and an interesting local folk museum. Don't leave without sampling Emmentaler cheese (see p. 148), renowned throughout Switzerland and beyond.

afar, in comfort; for the more adventurous, the glaciers could be seen at closer range. Poets such as Goethe, Byron, Shelley and Longfellow were captivated by these mountains, as were the composers Mendelssohn, Wagner and Brahms, and it's not difficult to see why.

A one-day excursion from Berne—either a guided tour or on your own—can cover some of the loveliest countryside in the Oberland. After all, the unofficial capital of the region, Interlaken, is just 53 kilometres by motorway from Berne.

Interlaken

This popular tourist centre lies at a modest altitude of 1,863 feet, "between the lakes" of Thun and Brienz, in sight of the Jungfrau massif. In the centre of the town is a vast prairie of a park, from which the unimpeded view of snow-dusted mountaintops inspires even the unsusceptible.

Interlaken has a permanent population of only about 13,000, but the town seems bigger than that during the summer when tourists in residence and in transit compete for café tables and parking space. Among the cultural

BERNESE OBERLAND

No other area of Switzerland offers so much to the tourist as the Bernese Oberland, the highlands south of Berne: majestic mountains, glaciers, waterfalls and lakes, plus scores of appealing villages and holiday resorts. Early in the 19th century—long before skiing and hiking developed into popular pursuits— the aristocrats of France and England flocked here to view the Jungfrau, from attractions here, appropriately, is a museum tracing the history of tourism in the region.

The most fashionable avenue in town is the **Höheweg,** known locally as the "Höhe", along which stand the great Victorian hotels, the restaurants and shops, and the casino *(Kursaal)* which has been the focus of social life here since 1859. The Höheweg, a long, straight, tree-lined boulevard, is ideal for strolling; you can also go along it in a horse-drawn carriage—looking up at the Jungfrau all the while. (Pedestrians who require still more exercise will find 50 kilometres of country paths in the vicinity, all clearly marked, with benches provided along the way.)

From Wilderswil near Interlaken a cog railway goes up the **Schynige Platte** for a superb view of the Bernese Alps. There's also a garden of Alpine blooms.

Lake of Thun

Vintage steamers ply the bigger, but shallower, of Interlaken's lakes, the **Thunersee** (Lake of Thun). Go for a boat trip, a drive or train ride along the shore. The villages teetering high above the lake, or nestled along the waterfront, add a man-made charm to the glory of the great outdoors.

Along the north shore a dramatically engineered road alternates between hillsides and lakeside, revealing resort villages and peaceful woodlands. The village of Oberhofen is notable for its medieval castle, remodelled and sumptuously decorated in the 17th and 19th centuries. Items from Berne's historical museum are on display. Reminiscent of the much more celebrated castle of Chillon (near Montreux), **Schloss Oberhofen** stands down by the water. An added attraction along the north shore is the view of the Alps across the lake.

The small town of **Spiez,** on the south shore, has an imposing **castle** dating from the 12th and 13th centuries. The museum within displays souvenirs of the one-time proprietors, as well as magnificent period furnishings.

Popular with yachtsmen, Spiez offers easy access to mountain resorts like Adelboden (see p. 70) and Kandersteg; the road up follows a delightful valley sprinkled with appealing villages and wooden farmhouses. Another road from Spiez branches off to Gstaad (see p. 70), where film stars and royalty jostle each other in the ski-lift queues.

From Mülenen, several kilometres south of Spiez, a funicular ascends the **Niesen,** an impressive look-out at 7,749 feet. **Thun,** a pleasant old town at the far end of the lake of the same name, has its own romantic castle. The history of the castle can be traced back to the end of the 12th century, when Duke Berchtold V of Zähringen defeated the barons of Thun, taking over the town and castle.

The setting of Thun is one of its charms: the core of the old town occupies a long, narrow and eminently walkable island in the River Aare, as it flows out of the lake. (The Aare traverses the lakes of Thun and Brienz). North of the river, an unusual city-planning scheme has turned **Hauptgasse,** the main street, into an intriguing shopping zone on two levels. You can walk on the flower-decked roofs of the streetside shops—alongside the upper level of shops. A covered stairway at the top of the thoroughfare goes up to the castle and Baroque parish church—from a point you could easily miss, hidden between houses number 55 and 57 in the Obere Hauptgasse.

Schloss Thun is a complex of fortifications crowned by a Romanesque square tower with four corner turrets. The **Historisches Museum** (Historical Museum), founded in 1888, occupies three floors of the keep. The main attraction is the Knights' Hall, a stately chamber in which are displayed an array of pikes and halberds and 15th-century tapestries. The floor above features Swiss army uniforms and weapons from the crossbow era to modern times, and the floor below, popular arts of the Oberland and a selection of 19th-century toys, dolls and doll houses.

Lake of Brienz

Interlaken's other lake, the **Brienzersee** (Lake of Brienz), has fewer resorts along its shores but no less inspiring scenery, best viewed from a paddle-wheel steamer. The town of **Brienz,** at the eastern end of the lake, is the centre of the Swiss woodcarving industry. If you buy a souvenir of carved wood almost anywhere in the Bernese Oberland, chances are it was fashioned in Brienz. The town boasts a school for woodcarvers and one for violin-makers, and, as you may imagine, no shortage of souvenir shops. Even the houses of Brienz have a hand-carved appearance.

Looming over the town is the **Brienzer Rothorn,** altitude over 7,700 feet. You can travel to the top aboard quaint old railway carriages propelled by a 19th-century steam locomotive (though diesel engines may also be put into service during the peak tourist period). This is the last steam-driven cog railway still operating in Switzerland. The hour-long trip up the Rothorn reveals scenes of tranquil, unpolluted beauty. From the terminus you have to walk to the summit (about 15 to 20 minutes away). The view stretches all the way around from the jagged peaks of the Alps to the distant Jura mountains.

A classic excursion by boat (or road) and funicular goes out to

Giessbach Falls. The cascades, 14 in all, rush down from a height of some 1,200 feet. A romantic spot if ever there was one, Giessbach has an old-fashioned honeymoon hotel.

Switzerland abounds in museums of folklore and ethnography, but none more ambitious than the **open-air museum** at Ballenberg, in the valley a few kilometres northeast of Brienz. The official name of the place is Schweizerisches Freilichtmuseum für ländliche Bau- und Wohnkultur, but all you have to say is "Ballenberg". Like Stockholm's pioneering open-air museum, Ballenberg groups actual village houses, some as many as three centuries

Flowers galore adorn a tidy chalet in lush central Swiss countryside.

old, transplanted to the site from various parts of the country. Their juxtaposition highlights regional variations in style, materials and methods of construction, enabling you to gauge the differences between, say, an Oberland chalet with its low-pitched roof and wide gables and a sober Valais farmhouse of masonry and wood. The interiors are authentically furnished: go inside for a closer look. Craftsmen are on hand to demonstrate traditional country skills.

Mountaineers, hikers and tourists frequent **Meiringen,** a pretty little town about 20 kilometres from Brienz on the upper reaches of the Aare. Fires in the late 19th century destroyed most of the historic buildings, but a few typical wooden structures survived.

While you're in the area you should see the deep **Aare Gorges,** a striking natural attraction. And don't miss **Reichenbach Falls,** reached by funicular, the scene of one of English literature's most dramatic fictional events: this is the waterfall where Sherlock Holmes and his arch-enemy Moriarty plunged to their "deaths".

From May or June to October, the postal bus departs from Meiringen for a circuit of three high mountain **passes**—the Susten, Furka and Grimsel—all well over 7,000 feet high. Grandiose scenery unfolds all along the way—a return journey of 133 kilometres.

To the Summits

Railway buffs and armchair mountaineers can scarcely resist the comfortable excitement of the trip from Interlaken to the Jungfraujoch, Europe's highest railway station at a dizzying altitude of 11,360 feet. On a clear day, this provides the view of a lifetime and

---

Cogs and Cable Cars

You can climb a Swiss mountain with crampons, pick and rope. Or you can do it the easy way, by rail or overhead transport. Cog-wheel railways have been the backbone of Swiss mountain travel since the 1870s. The line up the Pilatus, the steepest in the world, has been in operation since 1889.

Cable railways are different: the train has no engine of its own but is propelled along by a moving cable; the weight of the descending train balances that of the one moving upwards. About 50 of these lines still operate in Switzerland.

With overhead cableways, the most modern technology, even the cruelest terrain can be crossed. The highest line, from Zermatt to the Little Matterhorn, reaches more than 12,500 feet.

Experienced skiers who like to escape the crowds have yet another alternative: helicopters, now routinely used for charter ski jaunts.

the freshest air you'll ever inhale. But it's wise to check the weather forecast before undertaking the trip, lest the spectacular horizon be blotted out by fog or falling snow. Because of the altitude, no one suffering from heart problems should attempt the trip.

You can drive part of the way, but the roads run out at Grindelwald (see p. 70) or Lauterbrunnen, depending on which rail route you use. If you go all the way from Interlaken by train, you can ascend by one route and return by the other, for more varied sights.

Construction of the **Jungfraubahn** was one of the great technological achievements of the turn of the century, for the route tunnels a gradual spiral inside the storied Eiger, avoiding most of the perils of landslides and storms. In 1912 the top station was finally reached, 16 years after

the first spade-full of earth was turned on the foothills.

Whether you come from Grindelwald or Lauterbrunnen, you board the Jungfraubahn at **Kleine Scheidegg** station. Ahead looms the terrible north face of the Eiger (first conquered in 1938) and the soaring peaks of the Wetterhorn, Mönch and Jungfrau. The almost unbroken tunnel section, 7 kilometres long, begins after the station at Eigergletscher, where you

Three of the mightiest: sightseers take in (from left to right) Eiger, Mönch and Jungfrau peaks.

find yourself looking head on into the glacier. In summer, you see the moraine, the rocky debris that covers the ice, but early winter snows provide cosmetic camouflage. The train also stops twice, briefly, at Eigerwand and

Eismeer, so passengers can get out and peer through picture windows cut into the rock.

But the superlative is at the end of the line, at **Jungfraujoch,** where civilization has intruded in the unlikeliest place. There is a hotel, a restaurant and a viewing terrace which overlooks the Aletschgletscher, the longest glacier in the Alps. Wear warm clothing, even in summer, and put on appropriate footwear: if the weather's good you can go outside for walks through the snow (keep to signposted paths!) or rides in dog-sleds. Other attractions include visits to an "ice palace" of regal dimensions (near the railway station) and a small exhibition on the theme of high-altitude scientific research.

Another fair-weather outing for high-altitude travellers is the trip to the **Schilthorn,** a popular mountaintop vantage point. From the villages of Stechelberg and Mürren (see below), a cableway goes up to a revolving restaurant 9,744 feet above sea level. It takes 50 minutes for the turning platform to come full circle, allowing plenty of time for gazing out over the Bernese Alps, the Mont-Blanc, the Jura range, the Vosges chain and the mountains and valleys in between.

Before you leave the area, take in one more sightseeing "must": **Trümmelbach Falls.** A lift carries sightseers to lighted galleries be-low ground for a close look at the cascade as it pounds through subterranean gorges. Wear a raincoat.

Five Favourite Resorts

Adelboden. A sunny family resort in the Engstligen Valley, facing a glorious skyline. Renowned for its healthy climate. Bustling, small-town atmosphere; pleasant summer and winter.

Grindelwald. Not one but two glaciers come down to the edge of this lively international resort, popular the year round. Because it's accessible by car, Grindelwald attracts many day-trippers.

Gstaad. This fashionable resort combines scenery and social life. In summer: swimming, golf, tennis, horse riding and the Menuhin music festival.

Mürren. You can only reach Mürren by cable railway (from Lauterbrunnen) or cable car (from Stechelberg): because automobiles are banned, this resort on a balcony above the Lauterbrunnen Valley is quieter and cosier than most, though the relative inaccessibility may hamper excursion prospects.

Wengen. Bigger than Mürren across the valley but also free of cars, Wengen is an animated ski resort as well as a centre for summer relaxation. The situation, in full view of the Jungfrau, is exceptional. Accessible from Lauterbrunnen by cog railway.

LUCERNE AND CENTRAL SWITZERLAND

Just about all the elements of a perfect tourist town converge in Lucerne (*Luzern* in German): a superb waterfront setting against a backdrop of mountains; historic churches, interesting shops and plenty of greenery; an annual music festival; and paddle-wheel excursion boats. Lying at the geographical heart of Switzerland, Lucerne has been captivating travellers since before the invention of tourism.

The situation of the town has a good deal to do with it. Here the wide expanse of the Vierwaldstättersee (Lake of the Four Forest Cantons) narrows to become the swiftly flowing River Reuss. Medieval wooden bridges span the river, and ancient spires and towers fill the skyline. The shores of the wide blue lake are cradled by magnificent mountains; they plunge dramatically, or slope down to the waterside through green fields, woods and villages.

A thousand years ago, Lucerne was a tiny fishing village with a Benedictine monastery. The powerful Alsatian Abbey of Murbach held sway here. Under the abbots of Murbach, Lucerne developed into a market town, growing in importance with the opening of the Gotthard route across the Alps. The citizens enjoyed relative freedom until 1291, when control passed from the abbey to the Habsburgs. In 1332, in a move to shrug off Habsburg domination, Lucerne joined the fledgling Swiss confederation. After the confederate victory at the Battle of Sempach in 1386, an independent Lucerne prospered. A staunchly Catholic town, Lucerne led resistance to the Reformation.

By the 18th century Lucerne was the biggest town in the country (it now has a population of 64,000). This was the era when local men were being sent abroad as mercenary soldiers; at home, the patrician class flourished. Poets began to recognize the beauty of the mountains, and the first travellers arrived.

In the troubled year of 1846, when the Catholic cantons broke away from the confederation, Lucerne was in the forefront of the rebellion. With reconciliation, the town developed into a popular and peaceful resort.

Ornate hotels were built along the lakeshore; in 1870 the legendary Caesar Ritz opened the Grand Hotel National here and Auguste Escoffier took charge of the kitchen. Alexandre Dumas called Lucerne "a pearl in the world's most beautiful oyster". The town so enthralled Richard Wagner that he stayed for six years. "The sweet warmth of Lucerne's quay is such that it even makes me forget my music!", the composer exclaimed.

Lucerne

A likely starting point for any walking tour of old Lucerne is the railway station, which enjoys an overall view of lake, mountains, grand hotels, the river and the medieval city.

Switzerland's quintessential covered bridge, the **Kapellbrücke,** symbol of Lucerne, was built early in the 14th century. More than 100 gable paintings (17th century) of Lucerne's saints and heroes and of events in Swiss history decorate this span across the Reuss, reserved for pedestrians only. The octagonal stone tower alongside is called the **Wasserturm** (Water Tower). Until the 19th century it served as a prison, archives and treasury.

The twin-towered **Jesuiten-kirche** (Jesuit Church), a little further along the left bank, counts as one of the earliest (begun in the 1660s) and most beautiful Baroque buildings in Switzerland. The exuberant white and pink interior with its stuccowork and frescoes dates from 1750 and the towers from 1893.

Across the way lies the **Franzis-kanerkirche** (Franciscan Church), built before 1300 in high Gothic style. The stark lines of the interior accord with the ideals of poverty avowed by the mendicant order, though in later centuries many adornments were added, such as a richly carved pulpit and choir stalls.

Go back to the riverfront (site of the old arsenal or *Zeughaus*) and another covered bridge, the early 15th-century **Spreuerbrücke** (Mill Bridge). The paintings in the gables here, executed between 1625 and 1632, depict the *Dance of Death,* a perennial medieval theme.

Once across the river, you reach the most striking part of the old town: **Weinmarkt,** Lu-

cerne's thriving hub in the Middle Ages. Most of the buildings—once guildhalls, shops and mansions—have elaborately painted façades.

More ancient houses surround the flag-bedecked **Hirschenplatz,** the square where the hog market was held. Look for the sign of the historic Gasthof zum Hirschen (Stag Inn), a hostelry popular since the 15th century.

Between the river and the square called **Kornmarkt,** the impressive early 17th-century **Rathaus** (Town Hall) remains a vital centre of Lucerne life. The city council meets here, exhibitions are staged, and couples are married in its opulent rooms. The

Lucerne's 14th-century bridge is a picturesque landmark.

building successfully combines incongruous elements: a Swiss-style roof and Italian Renaissance façade.

The surrounding patrician houses consist of two sections connected by a multi-storey arcade. One of these houses, the beautiful Am Rhyn-Haus at 21 Furrengasse, contains the noted **Picasso Collection,** a display of late works.

The imposing houses of Rathausquai give onto the water. At the far end, in charming Kapellplatz, you'll come to the little Peterskapelle, a church built no less than 800 years ago.

Take one of the streets leading uphill, away from the river, to the **Museggmauer**—one of the best preserved and longest fortifications in Europe, illuminated at night during the tourist season. The wall, built about 600 years ago, originally enclosed the whole town. From May to October, part of the parapet and several of the towers are open to the public. There's a sweeping view of the town, the lake and the mountains.

A short walk from the wall by way of Museumplatz and Löwenplatz brings you to Lucerne's famous lion monument, the heroic **Löwendenkmal.** Mark Twain described it as "the most mournful and moving piece of stone in the world". The noble beast, depicted as mortally wounded by a spear, was designed by a Danish sculptor, Bertel Thorwaldsen, and carved out of the rock face in 1821. It honours Swiss mercenary soldiers who fell defending King Louis XVI during the French revolution: faithful to death, some 800 Swiss guards lost their lives in the storming of the Tuileries on August 10, 1792.

The nearby **Gletschergarten** (Glacier Garden) is an appealing park furnished with glacial potholes left by remnants of the retreating Ice Age, perhaps 20,000 years ago. A museum in the grounds provides useful background information on this geological phenomenon.

Heading down towards the lake you pass another attraction: the **Panorama** in Löwenplatz, a vast circular painting of 1889 illustrating the retreat of defeated French army units into internment in Switzerland during the Franco-Prussian War (1870–71). The young Ferdinand Hodler participated in the execution of the painting.

Near the lake in Leodegarstrasse stands the elegant **Hofkirche** (more properly the Collegiate Church of St. Leodegar and St. Mauritius), founded in the 8th century. The two slim towers date back to the 14th century, but the rest of the building was constructed anew after a fire in 1633. Tuscan-style arcades surrounding the church contain the tombs of Lucerne's great families.

Two Important Museums

Switzerland's most popular museum can be reached from the centre of town by car, bus or ferryboat. The **Verkehrshaus der Schweiz** (Swiss Transport Museum) on the Lucerne lakeside is one of the biggest and most comprehensive collections of its kind in Europe, and the first in the world to install a modern, four-engined jet passenger plane as a historic exhibit. (The Convair Coronado, retired by Swissair, had to be barged down the lake, laboriously, to its final resting place.)

The aeronautics section of the museum contains dozens of vintage planes, as well as a reconstruction of the control tower of Zurich airport. Exhibits on astronautics include original space capsules from early American flights and a fragment of lunar rock. There's also a planetarium. The department devoted to rail transport has more than 60 real engines on show (climb aboard!), plus the most elaborate model railway you're ever likely to see—a faithful reproduction in miniature of a section of the St Gotthard line.

Don't miss Swissorama, a 20-minute film on Switzerland's people, culture, traditions and economy projected on a circular screen. Spectators follow the action from a platform in the middle of the theatre. The museum also deals with the evolution of the motor car, tourism, postal and communications services, and navigation on rivers, lakes and seas. (Yes, landlocked Switzerland is a full-scale maritime nation, with a fleet of oceangoing cargo ships. Created at the beginning of World War II, the flotilla keeps in touch with Berne by radio.)

On the opposite shore of the lake, at Tribschen, the **Richard Wagner Museum** occupies the spacious house in which the composer lived from 1866 to 1872. It was here that he married Cosima, daughter of Franz Liszt. Set on a green promontory with a lovely view, the villa meant so much to Wagner that he vowed, "Nothing will make me leave this place". But at last he gave it up for Bayreuth.

On the main floor you can see a selection of original scores, letters and photographs, the composer's grand piano and his death mask. Upstairs is the municipal collection of old and exotic musical instruments, from bells to zithers.

Lucerne's Lake

To experience central Switzerland at its most delightful get out onto the **Vierwaldstättersee.** You can cruise the lake in style aboard "old world" steamers. Choose from any number of excursion trips on offer in the summer season.

With Mt. Pilatus (see p. 78),

Photo: Swissair

nearly 7,000 feet high, in the background, the gentle banks of the central plateau gradually give way to the lower Alps with their green pastures, while the great Alps loom imperiously over the water at the southern end of the lake.

On a typical excursion you sail past Küssnacht Bay, a bright, flowered scene of orchards and peak-roofed farmhouses. A chapel on the bay commemorates Queen Astrid of Belgium, who was killed here in a car accident in 1935.

The stretch of lakeside from Hertenstein to Brunnen is dotted with resort towns, lush gardens and villas. Towering over it all is Mt. Rigi (see p. 78), a favourite for hiking. You can go to the top by cable car and cog-wheel railway from the enchanting resort villages of **Weggis, Vitznau** and **Goldau.**

High above the lake on the other side perches **Bürgenstock**, once one of Europe's most fashionable resorts and still catering to a grand hotel style of tourism.

Before the ship pulls in at Brunnen, spare a glance for **Gersau**, a village with a momentous history. Before joining the canton of Schwyz in 1817, Gersau had been an independent republic, fiercely defending its sovereign rights for more than 400 years.

Pilot's-eye view to the south shows ring of mountains dominating city of Lucerne and its romantic lake.

After **Brunnen**, with its pleasant waterfront and glorious views, an 80-foot-high rock across the lake comes into view. This is the Schillerstein, dedicated to Friedrich

77

Schiller, the German dramatist whose romantic version of the William Tell story gave the Swiss hero belated fame around the world. (But Schiller never actually visited the area.)

Further on, a little green field with a solitary wooden house is the **Rütli**. This historic spot, where the Swiss confederation was born in the summer of 1291, symbolizes national unity. And in 1940, with Switzerland surrounded by the Axis powers, it was here that the commanding general, Henri Guisan, chose to rally his officers to the nation's defence.

Lake Uri is the most dramatic branch of the great lake, with its sheer cliffs plummeting into deep waters like a far northern fjord. Snow-capped mountains are silhouetted on the horizon.

On the east bank, **Tell's Chapel** marks the rock where William Tell is said to have leaped ashore on escaping from the boat carrying him to prison. Until the middle of the 19th century, it was the scene of waterborne religious and patriotic processions.

At **Flüelen,** formerly the staging post for mule trains crossing the Gotthard pass, you've reached the end of the lake. Behind this port is the capital of the canton of Uri, **Altdorf,** the place where Tell supposedly shot the apple and the site of Tellspielhaus, the theatre where Schiller's play is staged.

Three Mountains

Pilatus. Lucerne's most striking landmark was first climbed in the 16th century. This was no mean achievement at the time, and not only for the mountaineering skills required: local people considered the peak to be haunted by the evil spirit of Pontius Pilate (hence the name), and the mountain was off-bounds on pain of imprisonment. Then the lake where the spirit was thought to reside was drained, and Pilatus lost its ill repute. When mountain climbing became the fashion in the 19th century, the first inn was built here.

A popular way to visit is to take the boat or train to Alpnachstad, then the cog railway (with a maximum gradient of 48 per cent, the steepest in the world) to the top, nearly 7,000 feet. The summit, with its boundless views, is only a five-minute climb from the station. You can return to lake level by an alternate route, the cable car to Kriens.

Rigi. On a clear day the wide-angled prospect of the Alpine skyline from here reveals peaks as distant as the Jungfrau. The Rigi panorama from nearly 6,000 feet above sea level is one of Switzerland's great spectacles—and you don't have to be a mountain climber to enjoy it. This "island in the sun" may be reached by rail or lake steamer, then cog-wheel railway or aerial cable way.

Watching the sun rise over the

Alps is a mystical experience that can be witnessed from no better vantage point than the Rigi. One famous visitor was Mark Twain: reaching the top so exhausted him that he slept through the day and awoke just in time for the sunset.

Titlis. Nearly twice as high as the Rigi, this is central Switzerland's highest mountain at 10,627 feet. The ascent by funicular and cable car begins at the resort of Engelberg, 35 kilometres from Lucerne. At the Little Titlis summit—a perpetual deep-freeze —you can wander through an ice grotto and have lunch with a view of the nearer peaks of the Bernese Oberland and the Valaisan Alps. The cable car goes no higher, though mountaineers make it to the top of Titlis itself, a distance of 66 feet, in an hour or so. The town of **Engelberg** itself boasts a sunny setting and a sizable Benedictine monastery, founded in the 12th century and vastly expanded over the centuries. The Baroque abbey church is open to visitors.

East of Lucerne

Statistics show that the small canton of Zug is the richest per capita of all the cantons of wealthy Switzerland. The affluence of the cosmopolitan little capital city, also called **Zug**, has its romantic side in the almost perfectly preserved old town and the lakefront promenades, looking out on a smallish imitation of Geneva's fountain-in-the-lake.

Among international financiers Zug is well known as a tax haven, which explains the presence of so many company headquarters and sumptuous villas. But the charm of the town derives from its historic atmosphere and lakefront setting. Within the old town, you can roam three streets that conjure up medieval Switzerland—Fischmarkt, Untergasse and Obergasse. At the crossing of Fischmarkt and Untergasse stands the **Rathaus** (Town Hall), notable for its magnificent council chambers. Several remnants of the medieval fortifications survive, among them the **Zytturm** (Clock Tower) in Kolinplatz. Its startling tile roof of blue and white flaunts the colours of the canton.

St.-Oswalds-Kirche near by, built in the 15th and 16th centuries, is considered one of the country's outstanding late Gothic churches. Notice especially the finely sculpted details of the Royal Portal *(Königspforte),* the main entranceway. The figures of saints Oswald and Michael flank an expressive Virgin.

For a cantonal capital with a distinguished historical tradition, the town of **Schwyz**—which gave Switzerland its name and its flag—turns out to be a tranquil place, smaller than you might have imagined, in a pastoral setting. The most decorative building is the 16th-century Rathaus (Town Hall), with exterior murals (1891) depicting events in Swiss history. On the opposite side of the main square, the Baroque parish church of **St. Martin** has a richly adorned interior. Just down the street, the **Federal Archives Building** *(Bundesbrief-archiv)*, a modern white building with a bright contemporary fresco on the façade, contains irreplaceable documents from Switzerland's past. Here are kept the original compact of 1291 uniting the first three cantons (see p. 17) and subsequent charters by which the confederation was pieced together.

The biggest tourist attraction in the canton of Schwyz is the small town of **Einsiedeln,** chock-a-block with hotels. What brings the crowds here is not so much the beauty of the nearby forests or the good cross-country skiing: Einsiedeln is Switzerland's prime place of pilgrimage, a town physically and spiritually dominated by its historic church. The **Bene-dictine Abbey** dwarfs the civic buildings across the main square, presenting a certain asymmetry between church and state.

The story of Einsiedeln goes back more than 1,100 years to a monk named Meinrad, who was murdered in his hermit's cell in the forest. A century later he became a cult figure, and a fol-lowing of monks founded a monastery in his memory on the site of his martyrdom.

A tour de force of Baroque architecture, the abbey church and monastery buildings are regarded as the masterpiece of the architect Caspar Moosbrugger, a lay brother who lived at Einsiedeln for over 40 years. The **church,** with its sweeping façade and twin towers, lies at the centre of the vast ensemble. The gold and white interior is the celebrated work of the Asam brothers of Munich: Cosmas Damian painted the frescoes and Egid Quirin executed the stuccowork.

In the midst of this extravagant decoration, in a chapel marking the place where Meinrad met his death, stands a tiny Black Madonna—the goal of many pilgrims who believe she will answer their prayers.

Visitors may enter the monastery complex to view the **Fürsten-saal** (Hall of Princes), a richly decorated room filled with portraits of kings and popes. The name recalls a time before the 15th century when the abbots of Einsiedeln were princes of the German empire. Today Einsiedeln is a self-sufficient community of around 100 monks and 50 lay brothers, who work at trades ranging from mechanic to bricklayer to baker. The monastery also operates a printing shop, a horse stud and a cattle farm.

THE GRISONS

This unspoiled mountain district thrusting eastwards from the rest of Switzerland is the largest and most sparsely populated canton, and the only one where three languages are spoken: German, Italian and Romansh. Covering about one-sixth of the area of all Switzerland, the Grisons *(Graubünden)* is an up-and-down world of remote farms and villages scattered through craggy, irregular mountain chains. The Swiss themselves find it a great place for getting away from it all.

The history of the Grisons centres on its transalpine passes—and the triumph of man over mountain. Even in the jet age, several of the canton's ten main passes remain major arteries of European communication.

Among the first inhabitants to leave a lasting mark on the region were the Rhaetians, a tribe whose descendants still speak Romansh, Switzerland's fourth national language. Seeking command of the mountain passes, the Romans conquered the Rhaetians in A.D. 15, then colonized the region. Later the German emperors took control of the strategic passes, establishing hundreds of years of feudal rule.

In the 15th century, the people rebelled. They formed alliances like the Grey League *(Grauer Bund)*—from which the Grisons takes its name—and managed to escape from foreign and ecclesiastical domination. Outside pressures kept the sturdy mountaineers united, but their independence was difficult to defend against the buffeting of various European powers. In 1803, with a shove from Napoleon, they cast in their lot with the Swiss confederation.

Chur

The cantonal capital, a city of 35,000, is the traffic crossroads and regional gateway. From here you can branch out into several major regions: west via Flims towards the source of the Rhine; south over the Julier or Albula passes to St. Moritz and other famous Engadine villages; or north and east to Klosters and Davos. Travel by car or postal bus or on the narrow-gauge regional railway, the Rhätische Bahn.

Chur (pronounced Koor) is a thriving little city with modern shopping facilities, historic narrow streets, and squares of unusual shapes and moods. The local tourist authorities have laid out two sightseeing walks around town. All you have to do is follow the red or green footprints painted on the streets. They show the way to places of historic interest, although the markings are so unobtrusive you may occasionally lose the trail.

Look out for the ancient church of **St. Luzi** (St. Luzistrasse), noted for its 8th-century crypt, and the medieval Town Hall *(Rathaus)* in Poststrasse, three buildings in one.

A stone stairway and medieval gate tower lead to the castle on the hill, the Baroque **Bischöfliches Schloss**—a Bishop's residence that dates back to medieval times. It stands on a tranquil square surrounded by splendid mansions.

Opposite lies the **cathedral,** an eccentrically designed yet majestic Romanesque-Gothic church. (The floor tilts up towards the altar, and the chancel is out of alignment with the axis of the nave.) A huge 15th-century triptych of carved and gilded wood hangs above the altar. Ranged on either side are 13th-century statues of the apostles. The treasury, one of the richest in Switzerland, contains a collection of venerable reliquaries.

A fine late 17th-century house shelters the historical and folklore collections of the **Rhätisches Museum** (Hofstrasse 1), including costumes of the Grisons. The **Kunstmuseum** (Grabenstrasse 10) displays works of the 18th to 20th centuries by artists like the Grisons-born Angelica Kauffmann and the Giacometti family.

Cross-country competitors stride past in the Engadine ski marathon.

After you've seen the city sights, you may want to take in nearby **Maienfeld,** a charming village with some grand old patrician houses. It's just 15 or 20 minutes away by car. Maienfeld produces a dry, light red wine, the best in the area; happily, there are wonderful old inns in which to drink them. The Maienfeld region has another claim to fame: it provided the setting for *Heidi,* the children's book by Johanna Spyri, known around the world.

West from Chur

A scenic road follows the course of one of the Rhine's tributaries, the Vorderrhein (Outer Rhine), to its source near the Oberalp pass leading to Andermatt and the St. Gotthard. The route traverses heavily wooded country and the wide green Vorderrhein valley, where cows graze on summer grasses.

At the important road junction of **Reichenau** you'll see the spot where the two Rhine tributaries meet to form the great river which flows on through Switzerland to Germany, Holland and into the North Sea. The village's setting, on a forested "island" surrounded by the rivers, is strikingly beautiful.

The family resort of **Flims** is not one town but two: Flims-Dorf and Flims-Waldhaus, where the hotels are, surrounded by thick pine and larch forests dotted with sparkling lakes. A much smaller resort, **Laax,** has an interesting Baroque church (*Pfarrkirche*) dating from the 1670s; charming 19th-century chalets line the main street.

Ilanz proudly calls itself the first town on the Rhine. The claim is buttressed by many landmarks from its 1,200-year history. There are some distinguished houses here from the 16th and 17th centuries, like the grand Casa Gronda, but also a 20th-century 12-storey hotel that rather jars the historic atmosphere.

In **Trun,** stop and see the impressive 17th-century residence of the Disentis abbots, now a museum. An exhibition of local art and folklore adds to the interest of a visit.

Disentis (62 km. from Chur) is such a small country town that people put fences around their gardens to keep out the sheep. Yet it's also an ancient religious centre. A vast Benedictine **monastery** dominates the town and valleys all around. Founded 1,200 years ago, the monastery, one of the oldest in Switzerland, grew to great power in the Middle Ages. German emperors travelling east and west stayed overnight with the monks of Disentis, rewarding them with rich grants of land.

The present monastery complex dates from the 17th century, while the Abbey Church (*Klosterkirche*), raised over the grave of the hermit-monk, Sigisbert, took its present form at the beginning of the 18th century. Highlights of the splendid Baroque interior include eight elaborate side altars.

Beyond Disentis, you come to the **Oberalp pass,** an ancient Roman thoroughfare 6,700 feet high.

The Engadine

In the Engadine, the Valley of the River Inn (or En, as it is known here), the scenery is unique: high valleys reduce the impact of the Alpine peaks, bringing the mountaintops down to earth. But if the contrast in altitude is unremarkable, the levels of civilization run to extremes: for the Engadine encompasses some of the most simple and unaffected villages in Switzerland, as well as resorts of the utmost sophistication. And the villages, with their sturdy houses of stone construction, embellished with sgraffito* decoration, are unlike those of any other part of Switzerland.

The Engadine divides into two regions, upper and lower. The Upper Engadine extends from

Maloja to Zernez and is accessible from Chur via the Julier or Albula passes. St. Moritz, in the heart of the Upper Engadine, lies 77 kilometres from Chur. The Lower Engadine stretches from Zernez to Martina on the Austrian border and can be reached from Davos or Klosters by way of the Flüela pass.

Guarda, a protected national monument since 1939, faithfully preserves its aura of times past. Narrow cobbled streets, fountains with pinewood posts (an ancient fertility symbol) and buildings beautified by grillework, paint and sgraffiti make Guarda a worthwhile stop for anyone curious about local architecture and folklore.

Another fetching village is **Scuol** (Schuls in German), kingpin of a sprawling resort region that includes Tarasp and Vulpera. Scuol, "Spa Queen of the Alps", and Tarasp are thermal spas.

The lower town of Scuol, *Scuol sot* in Romansh, is an example of an Engadine village at its best. The houses display all the familiar elements of Engadine decoration: painted designs, sgraffiti, wrought iron balconies and window grilles. But the fountain in the main square is more than merely decorative; on the way to pasture the cows stop by to drink.

For a sweeping view of the Lower Engadine, ascend the Kreuzberg, just south-west of

---

* Sgraffito means "scratched" in Italian. The word is applied to designs scratched in a surface layer of wet plaster to reveal the contrasting colour of the layer underneath. In the Engadine, grey and white are the usual contrasting colours. Favoured motifs include rosettes, arabesques and scrolls.

Tarasp. The peak overlooks the impressive Schloss Tarasp with its 900-year-old chapel.

To the south-west, the mostly businesslike village of Zernez stands between the Lower and Upper Engadine. Zernez serves as the gateway to Switzerland's only **National Park** *(Parc Naziunal,* as the signs put it in Romansh). Don't expect an alpine Yellowstone or Yosemite; the park's area is only 62 square miles. Signs of civilization in this nature reserve are few and discreet, such as the well-marked hiking trails. The plant life is extremely varied, thanks to the big change in altitude from the valley floor to the

Mirror clear, the lake of Davos reflects a sunny, green hillside.

mountaintops; the animals, including ibex, chamois and stag, stay aloof from the tourists, but experienced nature-lovers can find and photograph them.

From here you can continue over the Ofen pass *(Pass dal Fuorn)* to **Müstair** (meaning "monastery" in Romansh), the principal village of the wooded valley of the same name on the Swiss-Italian border. At the time of the Reformation all the other towns in the area became Protestant, but Müstair, barricaded behind its monastery walls, kept the faith. The village is so rustic that stables and barns are strewn among the shops, hotels and houses along the main street.

Müstair's **Abbey of St. John the Baptist** was founded in the 8th century by the bishop of Chur, a relative of Charlemagne. (Tradition claims Charlemagne himself started the institution.) The historic abbey church with its triple apse underwent transformations in the 15th century. However, inside the church you can still see what may be the finest series of Carolingian **wall paintings** in the world. Created around the year 800, they depict the life and Passion of Christ, the crucifixion of St. Andrew and the Last Judgement. There is also a 12th-century statue of a full-bearded Charlemagne wearing his crown.

Back in the Inn Valley, **Zuoz** is a charmingly preserved village of the Upper Engadine with a fine church of original design. A group of attractive 16th- to 18th-century houses built by members of the Planta family surround the main square. Architectural attractions aside, Zuoz has also been developed as a resort.

Samedan's aerodrome, golf course and glider field help explain the popularity of this village as a year-round resort. So does its proximity to St. Moritz, just 7 kilometres away.

The only Engadine town with a world-wide reputation, **St. Moritz** (population 6,000) caters to a dynamic, cosmopolitan and very rich clientele. Even by Swiss standards, the shop windows here shimmer with luxury. You can buy everything from jewellery and furs to works of art.

The success of St. Moritz —which calls itself the birthplace of alpine winter sports (1884) —may be attributed to its dry sunny climate, the favoured natural setting, elaborate recreational facilities and a carefully cultivated reputation for elegance. The town is roughly divided in two: "Bad" (meaning spa or baths), the district around the lake, and, up the hill, "Dorf", with its palatial hotels.

The **Engadine Museum** displays typical furniture, tile stoves and historic weapons in a building based on regional architectural style, while the **Segantini Museum** exhibits works of the Italian landscape painter Giovanni Segantini (1858–99).

North-east of town, the belvedere of **Muottas Muragl** (a funicular goes to the top) dominates the whole of the Upper Engadine. Look down at Pontresina (see p. 90), out over the lakes of Sils (the retreat of Friedrich Nietzsche) and beyond to the Maloja Pass.

The trip from St. Moritz to the Bernina pass is impressive by car, bus or train. Among the sights, by road or rail: the glacier landscape of the **Morteratsch** and the **Diavolezza** and the alpine garden of **Alp Grüm**. Down at the village of Poschiavo, officially part of the Grisons, the stately main square is really a piazza. You can almost feel Italy just across the border.

Seven Alpine Resorts

Arosa. This stress-free resort 30 kilometres from Chur is most easily reached via narrow-gauge railway. Two small lakes reflect the hotels, chalets and pine-clad mountains. Worth visiting summer or winter.

Davos. A lively architectural mix of villas, chalets and hotels follows the long, winding main street from Davos Platz up to Davos Dorf. By far the biggest of the Grisons ski resorts. Famous as the setting of Thomas Mann's *Magic Mountain*.

Flims. This old established resort is especially well provided with hotel beds and holiday flats.

Decorated walls and windows warm a wintry street scene in Zuoz.

Accessible from Chur and Ilanz by postal bus. Skiing of all levels, plus summer bathing in the limpid Caumsee.

Klosters. Smaller, more fashionable resort than nearby Davos. In the Prättigau valley. Although it's packed with jet-setters in winter, Klosters has retained its village atmosphere.

Lenzerheide-Valbella. Twin resorts on opposite sides of a moun-

tain lake. Less known abroad than its competitors, Lenzerheide strives to attract year-round vacationers. Summer windsurfing and good hiking possibilities.

Pontresina. A fashionable ski centre just off the road to the Bernina pass. The smallest of the well-known Grisons resorts, Pontresina is on the Engadine cross-country ski trail. Summertime rambling and mountaineering.

St. Moritz. This glamorous resort offers a host of exciting winter-time activities, from sleigh rides, bobsleigh and skeleton competitions to golf and horse-racing on the frozen lake. In addition to varied downhill runs, St. Moritz also provides excellent cross-country skiing opportunities. A summer resort, as well, with sailing, golf and outdoor concerts.

TICINO

In the Ticino, Switzerland's southernmost canton, you bask in the sun and charm of neighbouring Italy, surrounded by Italian conversation, music... and food. It might almost be Italy but for the Swiss flags and the oversupply of banks—and the cleanliness, law and order, and general efficiency that sets Switzerland apart.

For international tourists the lure is the canton's southern lakeland and its renowned resorts fragrant with magnolia, mimosa and eucalyptus. But beyond the resorts, in the steep valleys of the Ticino, you can discover an almost-forgotten land of small farms separated by stone fences, with rough stone houses, teetering campaniles and little wayside chapels.

Milan is closer than Berne, so the Italian connection is strong, especially culturally. But the Ticino has been part of Switzerland since the 16th century and a full-fledged Swiss canton since 1803. These venerable links with the confederation are remarkable, considering that the canton was isolated from the rest of the country every winter until little more than a century ago, when the St. Gotthard railway tunnel was built. (A tunnel for motor vehicles was opened only in 1980.) The Ticino population slightly exceeds a quarter million, of whom an unusually high proportion—28 per cent—are foreigners. More than one in ten of the canton's permanent residents are German-speakers.

Bellinzona, the political capital of the Ticino, guards the way to

The lookout point atop Monte San Salvatore, Lugano's "Sugar Loaf", offers a soaring perspective.

three Alpine passes—St. Gotthard, Lukmanier and St. Bernardino. Thus the town has had a stormy history, its strategic position fought over by Romans, Franks, Lombards and Swiss. In a canton composed of small towns and villages, Bellinzona's population of 17,000 is by no means trivial; the animation of the Saturday morning street market attains almost metropolitan proportions.

Exploring the centre of town is a brief but rewarding adventure amid Lombard arches, balconied pastel-coloured houses and historic churches. The cobbled streets give way to piazzas large or small, often eccentrically shaped. But the unique sights of Bellinzona are the crenellated **walls**, parts of which pop up all over town, and three medieval castles.

Construction of the oldest castle, **Castel Grande** or Castel Vecchio may have begun under the Romans as long ago as the 4th century. Two tall medieval towers still stand. Built between the 13th and 15th centuries, **Castello di Montebello** was restored in 1903 and renovated in the 1970s to create an archaeological and historical museum, the Museo Civico. Here are shown discoveries from archaeological sites around the canton—ancient jewellery, ceramics and furnishings—and works of art and technology from more recent centuries.

The highest of the citadels, **Castello di Sasso Corbaro,** dates from the 15th century. It was built in some six months of day and night labour by order of the Duke of Milan, who feared an imminent offensive by the Swiss. The cantonal Museum of Popular Arts and Traditions has been installed in part of the dungeon. From the ramparts you can see as far as Lake Maggiore. Bellinzona's three forts are still referred to as the castles of Uri, Schwyz and Unterwald—names that go back to the 16th century when bailiffs representing the Swiss forest cantons ruled here.

Locarno and Lake Maggiore 🚶

Due west of Bellinzona on Lake Maggiore, **Locarno** luxuriates in subtropical foliage. There are orange trees, banana plants, slim date palms, and a year-round profusion of flowers. With an altitude of only 673 feet above sea level, Locarno is the least lofty town in Switzerland—not that mountains aren't near at hand.

A five-minute funicular ride from the centre of town leads to Locarno's best-known monument, the sanctuary of the **Madonna del Sasso.** Or, like the pilgrims who have come here for hundreds of years to pray at the site of a miraculous vision, you can climb the hillside on foot. From afar the church, perched on a steep rock, looks quite large, but inside it retains an air of intimacy. From the church you can continue uphill by cable car and chair lift to the summit of the **Cimetta,** a superb belvedere overlooking the town and the lake.

History and art attract visitors to Locarno's medieval castle, **Castello Visconti,** partly restored in the 1920s. The 15th-century arcaded courtyard indicates the former grandeur of the fortification, but only a fraction of the original complex has survived. Nowadays the building houses the Museo Civico, a rich archaeological collection that includes many Roman relics, and a gallery of contemporary art, largely a collection donated by the sculptor Jean Arp, a founder of Dada and a leading surrealist. An honorary citizen of Locarno, Arp died in the town in 1966.

With its open-air cafés, the main square of Locarno, **Piazza Grande,** a few streets from the castle, is the logical place to take a break and plan the day's further activities. The unique curved shape of this spacious square is explained by the historic lie of the land: the lake originally came right up to the north side of what is now the plaza; at the end of the 19th century, marshes and swamps to the south were filled in. The arcaded plaza serves as the site of Locarno's annual International Film Festival; films are projected onto an outdoor screen.

Uphill from here is the **Città Vecchia,** the old town of stately villas, time-worn tenements, hidden gardens and venerable churches. The mansions, designed with a southern flair, flaunt towers, turrets and other fanciful adornments.

Lake Maggiore extends from Switzerland into Italy. The lake is often awash with water-skiers, windsurfers, yachtsmen and sightseeing boats. A highlight of nautical tours is a stop at the **Isles of Brissago,** which are surrounded by shallow, translucent water. Flourishing on the larger island of San Pancrazio, given over to a **botanical garden,** are such exotic plants as bamboo, sugar-cane, cactus and all manner of citrus trees. Some tours continue in the direction of Stresa to the Borromeo Islands, in Italian waters.

The River Maggia's channel into the lake marks the dividing line between Locarno and its small but sophisticated neighbour, **Ascona.** This sunny resort, formerly a simple fishing village, has long attracted artists and intellectuals—including Isadora Duncan, Paul Klee and the exiled Lenin. Frequent art exhibitions and an annual festival of classical music make the town something of a cultural centre.

Ascona's equivalent of a main square stretches along the lakefront, assuring plenty of room for outdoor restaurants and cafés, as well as a tree-shaded **waterfront promenade.** The ferryboats dock right in the centre of town. Inland, the cobbled back streets have a Mediterranean air. Many of the charming old buildings have been converted into shops selling Swiss watches and jewellery, Swiss and Italian fashions, regional handicrafts and antiques. The town has its share of historic churches like Santa Maria della Misericordia, which preserves an important late Gothic fresco cycle.

To get the feel of the countryside, go out to **Ronco,** a few kilometres west, a picturesque village set high above the lake. Popular day-trips from Locarno and Ascona explore the isolated valleys above. The most rustic, **Val Verzasca,** may be reached by car, postal bus or organized excursion coach. It's just 31 kilometres from Locarno to the most distant village, **Sonogno,** but the contrast from the prosperous, sophisticated lakeside scene is almost total. Here the simple houses are all of stone; just one stone balanced on another; even the roofs are covered over with stones.

Organized excursions visit another, bigger valley, the **Valle Maggia,** which follows the twists and turns of the River Maggia on its way to the lake. Italianate architecture in all its variations is universal—until you reach the wooden chalets of the remote village of **Bosco** *(Gurin* in German), in a side valley settled in the 12th century by emigrants from the canton of the Valais. They still speak an obscure Swiss-German dialect.

Lugano and its Lake

First town of the Ticino with a population of some 30,000 and its most fashionable resort, **Lugano** sweeps down to a leafy lakefront promenade, backed by stately hotels, banks and office buildings. Excursion boats and yachts ply the lake. Its labyrinthine reaches and steep wooded shores create drama, and the villages up and down the slopes radiate character and charm.

In the parks and gardens for which Lugano is known, springtime comes early. Forsythia and mimosa flower in February; March brings camellia, magnolia and peach blossoms; and April is brightened by azalea, rhododendron, wisteria and Japanese cherry blossoms.

Lugano's main square, **Piazza della Riforma,** was designed on the scale of Italian grand opera; it's big enough for multiple ranks of outdoor café tables. You could sit by the hour at a table here, sipping an *espresso* or an *aperitivo* and watching the "beautiful people", and others, stroll past. Leading off from the square, arcaded shopping streets offer shelter from sun and rain.

Facing the lake a short distance south of the main square, the small church of **Santa Maria degli Angioli** is enriched by the finest Renaissance frescoes in the Ticino. The best known cycle, painted at the beginning of the 16th century, is Bernardino Luini's luminous version of Christ's Passion, which covers the tall partition dividing the choir and nave. Notice, too, Luini's Virgin and Child with St. John, decorating one of the chapels. A lakeside park across the busy avenue in front of the church displays a quantity of modern sculpture.

Lugano's **Cathedral** *(San Lorenzo)*, halfway up the hill from the lake to the railway station, is noted for its elaborate Renaissance façade with three harmoniously decorated portals. From the plaza in front of the church there is an appealing panorama of the town and its lake.

Unchallenged as Lugano's top attraction for art lovers is the 17th-century **Villa Favorita,** the residence of Baron von Thyssen-Bornemisza, a member of the German steel family. The mansion stands in its own lakefront park in Castagnola to the east of town. The collection of paintings and sculpture amassed by the baron has been called the biggest private art hoard in Europe. Happily, the public is admitted during the tourist season (but only at certain times; be sure to check with the Lugano tourist office). Some of the old masters (mainly German and Flemish) may be on loan to museums elsewhere, but you're likely to see an absorbing selection of paintings by Memling, Hans Holbein the Elder and Younger, Rubens, Hals, Van Dyck and, closer to the Ticino, Ghirlandaio, Raphael, Titian, Tintoretto and Caravaggio. The collection also includes rarely seen Impressionist and modern works.

An enthusiastic copy-writer once pronounced Lugano the "Rio de Janeiro of Europe" because of the way Monte San Salvatore rises from the lake Sugar Loaf-style. You can see the basis for this fantasy by taking the two-stage funicular to **Monte Brè,** to the east. At around 3,000 feet, it is not really much of a mountain, but the air is fresh and clear and the view of the hills reflected in the lake has undeniable glamour. **Monte San Salvatore** itself affords stunning mountain views. For ramblers there are pleasant paths to town from the top.

Boat trips on the Lake of Lugano offer relaxation, views of the hills tumbling down to the shore, and a chance to visit or at least glimpse some very pretty villages. Among the highlights:

Gandria. Many artists have been attracted to this unspoiled, flower-bedecked fishing village. Nearby is the **Museo Doganale**

Svizzero (Swiss Customs Museum), best reached by boat direct from Lugano. Anyone who has ever sneaked a bottle of perfume past a customs man will be interested to study the display of ingenious hiding places used by professional smugglers—all nabbed by Swiss customs officers, of course.

Melide, south of Lugano, may be reached by land or lake. Since 1959 this village has attracted millions of visitors as the home of **Swissminiatur,** an exhibition of more than 100 of the nation's principal man-made sights, modelled at $1/25$ the actual size. Chil-

The docking facilities are primitive in unspoiled Gandria, where nothing separates the village from the lake.

dren can't resist staring at the complex network of model trains, cars and even ships. Every detail of the cityscape is in scale except for the itinerant birds.

Morcote, at the tip of a hilly peninsula running south from Lugano, is a charming village of arcaded, stucco houses with red tile roofs. A long 18th-century stairway of stone leads up the steep hillside to the medieval chapel of Sant'Antonio Abate. Farther up, a tall, slender bell tower marks the **church** of Sta. Maria del Sasso and, among tall cypress trees, a large cemetery where, legend says, the spirits of Morcote people who died abroad come home on the night of November 2 (All Souls' Day).

From Capolago, the southernmost lake port in Switzerland, a cog railway mounts to **Monte Generoso** 5,595 feet high. The terrace at the top offers a unique view of the Lombardy plain to the south and, to the north, the lakes and hills of Ticino and the peaks of the Alps beyond. There is a restaurant near the summit, but otherwise little encroachment on this well-defended beauty spot.

The main motorway and rail routes from Frankfurt to Milan reach the Italian frontier at Chiasso, a Swiss town chock-a-block with banks and international commercial and transport companies. The customs men here keep very busy.

Campione d'Italia

Surrounded by Switzerland, Campione d'Italia is an enclave of Italy fraught with anomalies. The flag is Italian but the telephones are Swiss. The policeman lounging in the main square has a white helmet and that relaxed Italian stance, but his patrol car bears Swiss licence plates. The red post box is Italian, but if your letter is addressed to Switzerland, use a Swiss stamp.

If you arrive from the Ticino by road, you pass through the striped ceremonial arch of Campione d'Italia without so much as a glance from an official. Nor are there formalities if you come by excursion boat—25 minutes from Lugano to the shady side of the same lake.

Aside from the ambiguous pleasure of feeling neither in Italy nor Switzerland, the lure for tourists is Campione's lakeside gambling casino, built by Mussolini in 1933. Enthusiasts of roulette and chemin de fer converge at discreet tables illuminated by fringed lamps and crystal chandeliers. (Gentlemen are required to wear jacket and tie.) Campione is well known on the high-rollers' circuit of Europe. It became notorious in 1983 when Italian carabinieri and finance police raided the village in response to charges that the casino was controlled by the Mafia.

VALAIS

Since prehistoric times the long, dramatic valley called the Valais (*Wallis* in German) has been an important route between north and south Europe—and east and west. The lifeline is the River Rhone, which flows from the Rhone Glacier to the shore of Lake Geneva. On either side soar some of the highest peaks in the Alps.

The Alps block out the cold winds and much of the rain, while the orientation of the valleys in the path of the *föhn,* a warm, dry wind (see box, p. 135), gives the region a mellow climate conducive to the cultivation of fruit —including grapes for wine —and to leisure pursuits. One side valley is different from another, and each has its own costumes and traditions. Halfway through the canton, near the town of Sierre, the language suddenly changes from French to Swiss-German. But despite the linguistic division, the Valais remains united, thanks to the predominance of the Catholic religion.

We survey this land of historic churches and monasteries from west to east, from Saint-Maurice to the source of the Rhone.

The Lower Valais

Situated between a precipitous cliff and a range of mountains, **Saint-Maurice** may not appeal to the claustrophobic. But it is a precious storehouse of religion and art. The **Abbaye de St-Maurice** counts among the oldest monastic institutions in Christendom. Relays of monks, and later canons, have been singing psalms here without a break for perhaps 14 centuries. All this fervour commemorates a Roman army officer, Maurice, whose conscience kept him from obeying orders. Because he refused to worship the gods of Rome, Maurice and his followers—over 6,000 members of the Theban Legion—were massacred around the year 285.

Since the 4th century pilgrims (among them princes of Christendom) have been coming to this spot to leave offerings at the tombs of the martyrs. The **treasure** they bestowed lies locked behind three high-security doors inside the basilica of St-Maurice. Taped commentary describes the pieces of greatest rarity, beginning with three large reliquaries displayed in glass cases in the middle of the vault. The reliquary bust of St. Candidus, in silver, dates from the 12th century. But the oldest item is a **sardonyx vase,** an exquisitely carved pre-Christian container decorated with scenes from Greek mythology; the gold and precious stones were added in the 7th century.

Because of the small area of the vault and a lack of supervisory personnel, only a limited number of visitors can be accommodated inside the treasury at any one time. To be sure of seeing the collection, telephone in advance (025) 65 11 81.

The Rhone makes a sharp right-angle turn at **Martigny,** a crossroads town of significance since ancient times. The Roman amphitheatre (now a ruin) could seat 6,000 spectators. On a stark hillock overlooking the town, the gloomy tower of a 13th-century château has been restored. On the outskirts, striking modern architecture marks the Fondation Pierre-Gianadda, embracing museums of Roman antiquities and of the automobile, as well as a cultural centre which organizes interesting temporary exhibitions.

Travellers in a hurry take the toll tunnel, 6 kilometres long, linking Switzerland and Italy. Opened in 1964, it bypasses the worst hazards of the **Grand St-Bernard** (Great St. Bernard) pass, the classic route across the Alps, more than 8,000 feet high. The new road also side-steps the famous hospice founded around 1045 by St. Bernard of Menthon. If you have time to make the detour, visit the chapel with its richly carved 17th-century pulpit and stalls. The historical museum enshrines mementoes of Napoleon Bonaparte's trek across the pass in 1800 with an army of 40,000, on the way to the battle of Marengo. In the kennels behind the hotel you can see the brown-and-white dogs that used to ferret avalanche victims out of the snow. The portly dogs and the monks who worked with them maintained a tradition of rescue for more than nine centuries.

Sion

The landscape here is simply spectacular: the Alps all around, the Rhone coursing past, and in the middle of it all two hills rising up from the valley floor, each with a medieval citadel.

Nearly 1,000 years ago Sion added political and religious authority to its military significance. The bishops of Sion were given sweeping powers over the people of their diocese, encompassing the whole of the Valais. The best-remembered bishop, Cardinal Matthew Schiner (1465–1522), is a national hero notwithstanding his wheeling and dealing and occasional errors of judgement. (It was Schiner who urged the confederation to form an alliance with the pope, which led to conflict with France and the defeat of Swiss troops at Marignano.)

Starting with the twin hills of Sion: atop Tourbillon, the one nearer the mountains, are the ruins of a 13th-century episcopal castle. Valère, closer to the river, supports a formidable fortress-church. If you're rushed or too tired to climb two hills, choose

Valère. There is much to see in the Romanesque-Gothic church (the former cathedral): naïve stone carving, 15th-century frescoes and 17th-century choir stalls. The organ in this church, built in 1395 and still in use, is considered the oldest playable organ in the world.

Between the hills, in Rue des Châteaux, **La Majorie,** former residence of church officials, houses the Musée Cantonal des Beaux-arts, featuring paintings of Sion and the people of the Valais. Across the street, the modern **Musée Cantonal d'Archéologie** (Cantonal Archaeological Museum) displays objects excavated in the Valais.

Down in the town itself, see the 17th-century Town Hall *(Hôtel de Ville)*, painted pink. The astronomical clock in the belfry dates from 1667. The **cathedral** *(Notre-Dame-du-Glarier)*, a late Gothic structure, was put up after fire destroyed the original Romanesque edifice. Only the belfry survived the conflagration.

Finally to the 16th-century **Maison Supersaxo** just off the street of the same name: Georgius Supersaxo was the Latin name affected by Jörg auf der Flüe, a Valaisan who spent most of his life in contention with Cardinal Schiner. Father of 23 children, Supersaxo built this mansion to house his numerous family and to flaunt his wealth in the face of the

cardinal. The sculpted ceilings in the great hall are admirably overdone.

Sion is a good starting point for excursions into the surrounding mountains (accessible by postal bus). Off to the north are resorts like Crans/Montana (see p. 106) and Anzère. On the south side, the **Val d'Hérens** is noted for its picturesque villages of dark wooden houses generously embellished in summer with red geraniums. In the area around Evolène, women wear their traditional black-skirted costumes, even while working in the fields. Beyond is Arolla, a centre for mountaineering.

At the end of the **Val d'Hérémence** looms the world's highest concrete dam, the Grande-Dixence. Nearly a mile and a half above sea level, this triumph of engineering amid stunning scenery produces clean, cheap electricity on a massive scale. Enough concrete was poured into the dam, it's said, to build the Great Pyramid of Egypt twice over.

Heading east along the Rhone, you'll see signs in French/German indicating "Sierre/Siders". A last bastion of the French language, **Sierre** is entirely sur-

Valais village girls in festive finery scamper over the cobblestones.

rounded by vineyards. There are ample facilities for sampling the wines that result. Thanks to a particularly dry climate, Sierre can almost guarantee visitors a sunny stay.

The unspoiled **Val d'Anniviers**—a detour south of the Rhone—climbs to one of Europe's highest year-round inhabited villages, Chandolin, as well as charming mountain resorts such as St-Luc, Grimentz and Zinal, dominated by the Weisshorn and Zinalrothorn.

Beyond Sierre, in the valley of the Rhone, **Leuk** *(Loèche)* has a good number of historic châteaux and towers once occupied by officials representing the bishops of Sion. The upland spa of **Leukerbad** *(Loèche-les-Bains)*, a major centre for hiking and mountain climbing, stands at the end of the Gemmi Pass, a popular alpine crossing from Kandersteg.

From Gampel (between Sierre and Brig) a road leads steeply upwards into the **Lötschental,** a wild, high alpine valley isolated during the winter months until 1913, when the 15-kilometre-long railway tunnel from Goppenstein to Kandersteg was completed, linking the Valais and Bernese Oberland.

Women wear their costumes to work around the house in Les Haudères.

The Upper Valais

That magnificent mountain, the **Matterhorn,** is not the highest of alpine peaks, just the most impressive. Its famous pyramidal silhouette still challenges climbers from around the world. On average the Matterhorn continues to claim about a dozen lives every year. But, then, as many as 60 climbers attempt the ascent on any summer day.

The expedition that first reached the summit, 14,688 feet, was organized by a young Englishman, Edward Whymper. The assault on the north-east ridge—anxiously watched from below—succeeded on July 14, 1865. But the mystique of the peak was soon reinforced: on the way down, four members of the triumphant seven-man party plunged to their deaths.

Headquarters for assaults on the Matterhorn *(Mont Cervin* in French) is the celebrated resort town of **Zermatt,** situated at the end of a long side valley that extends for 37 kilometres from Visp. All mountain towns tend to be tightly knit communities, but Zermatt's closed corporation of citizens, formally called the *Burgergemeinde,* has been penetrated by only one "foreign" family in the past three and a half centuries. The Burgergemeinde owns the forests, pasture lands and various hotels of Zermatt.

Popular **Saas-Fee,** another high-altitude resort, lies in the valley parallel (see p.106).

Other Swiss towns may have mixed feelings about Napoleon Bonaparte, but **Brig** named a street after him. It salutes the military genius who built the Simplon route across the Alps, which begins here. For many travellers Brig is just a place to change trains or fuel the car. But a couple of buildings here are worth seeing.

In this town of towers and turrets, the domes of **Stockalper Castle** stand out. Baron Kaspar Jodok von Stockalper (1609–91), the most successful man of affairs in Valais history, wanted it that way. At the time of its construction, this ostentatious residence was the largest private house in Switzerland, with an arcaded courtyard big enough to serve as the warehouse for a transalpine shipping service, one of Stockalper's monopolies. A regional museum on the premises presents Valais crafts and customs.

Nearby, the Brig parish church provides a startling contrast to Stockalper's presumptuous project. Inside a simple modern building (1970), the white altarpiece beneath a black tent-like ceiling proves dazzlingly effective.

Just west of Brig, a 16th-century clock tower announces an unexpectedly big and ornate church in the suburb of Glis. It has a magnificent Italianate

porch and other Gothic, Renaissance and Baroque features.

The scenic route to Italy is across the **Simplon pass** (altitude 6,578 feet), 25 kilometres south of Brig. Motorists in a rush, or worried by the weather, can put their car on a train through the Simplon tunnel, which bores nearly 20 kilometres through the Alps.

The **Furka pass,** altitude 7,976 feet, is a vital link between western and eastern Switzerland. Just

before the top of the pass, you can stop at the **Rhone Glacier,** as impressive a mountain phenomenon as you'll see at close range. An ice grotto cut into the glacier provides an additional attraction for tourists. A railway tunnel 15 kilometres long now undercuts the Furka and ends the historic isolation of villages of the Goms Valley, hitherto cut off from central Switzerland for seven or eight months of the year.

Skiers and sightseers float across blinding white mountains. On the skyline: Valais and Bernese Alps.

Five Valais Resorts

Champéry. Families like this small resort with a village atmosphere. You can ski over the border to France. Neighbouring French and Swiss resorts pool ski lifts and runs. Otherwise, skating, curling, tennis, swimming with the Dents du Midi mountains in view.

Crans/Montana. Actually five towns join forces to make up Switzerland's biggest ski area, with accommodation for as many as 30,000 vacationers in hotels and chalets. Chic and modern, frequented by the international set. Summer skiing on the Plaine-Morte glacier. Golf and tennis.

Saas-Fee. A fashionable crowd favours this charming resort, surrounded by giant peaks. Until 1951, the village could only be reached by mule-train; cars are still banned inside the town. The underground funicular from Felskinn to Mittelallalin—the world's most lofty—ascends to the vertiginous height of nearly 11,500 feet.

Verbier. A cosy village atmosphere remains amid encroaching skyscrapers. Principally a winter resort with slopes for all kinds of skiers, from novice to professsional. Youth-orientated and trendy.

Zermatt. This famous resort, five kilometres from the nearest car, offers old-fashioned charm, modern comforts and year-round skiing. Taxi, mini-bus and train services operate from the car park in Täsch. Horse-drawn carriages and electric carts circulate in town. A cog-wheel railway goes up the Gornergrat, while Europe's highest cableway reaches the Little Matterhorn, 12,533 feet.

VAUD AND THE LAKE OF GENEVA

The French-speaking canton of Vaud, western Switzerland's most populous state, attractively combines industry and agriculture, history and contemporary life style. If the panoramas are less dramatic than the glaciers and waterfalls of the neighbouring Valais, there's compensation in the view of vineyards rising steeply from the biggest lake in the Alps.

Lac Léman, otherwise known as the Lake of Geneva, has long fascinated poets, artists, composers, as well as geographers and statisticians. The crescent-shaped lake covers an area of nearly 225 square miles; about three-fifths of it belongs to Switzerland, two-fifths to France.

On this mini-sea, towering waves can suddenly spring up. Captains of pleasure boats are always on the alert for perilous winds. But much of the time it's clear sailing on the Léman: a pageant of brightly striped spinnakers billow under a pale sky cross-hatched with jet trails; white lake steamers manœuvre among motorboats, canoes, windsurfers and self-confident swans and ducks. Ashore, holidaymakers and local people politely vie for seats under the parasols of the outdoor cafés, where tiny glasses are filled and refilled with the local white wine—an appropriate salute to the glorious convergence here of mountains, lake and sky.

Sights inland in the canton of Vaud are treated in the following chapter, pages 116 to 128.

La Côte

With a view across the Lake of Geneva to the French Alps, the towns and villages of La Côte are dotted along the lake shore from the edge of Geneva eastwards to the busy university and commercial city of Lausanne, a distance of 60 kilometres. If you drive from town to town, take the lake road which parallels the water, rather than the motorway further inland. Beyond Nyon begins the wine-growing region of La Côte. You can follow the signposted Route du Vignoble (Route of the Vineyards) up gently terraced hillsides. Some highlights along the coast:

Coppet. This pleasant village of arcaded stone houses evokes the image of the French writer Germaine Necker, better known as Mme de Staël. Her father, a Geneva banker, acquired the **château** of Coppet (now a museum) in 1784. A marble statue of the gentleman stands in the entrance hall. Portraits and memorabilia of his daughter are scattered through rooms decorated in Louis XVI and Directoire style. When Napoleon Bonaparte exiled Mme. de Staël from Paris in 1803, she took up residence in Coppet, accompanied by some of the leading figures of the Romantic movement. As one of her circle, the aristocratic philosopher Charles-Victor de Bonstetten observed: "More wit is dispensed at Coppet in one day than in the rest of the world in a year."

Nyon. The historic centre of Nyon encompasses Roman remains, a castle begun in the 12th century, a church of the same era and dozens of exemplary houses from the 15th to 19th centuries.

The five-towered **castle** of Nyon was designed and used as a military bastion by the expansionist dukes of Savoy, based across the lake; for an idea of life in Nyon in the Middle Ages, visit the château's history museum. The Roman mosaic in the courtyard recalls Nyon's founding by Julius Caesar around the year 45 B.C. Upstairs, a separate museum is devoted to the porcelain produced in Nyon in the late 18th and early 19th centuries.

Near the château in rue Maupertuis lie the remains of a Roman basilica of the 1st century A D. The ancient building, which has been enclosed, houses a museum of Roman artefacts—amphoras, mosaics, coins, glass, pottery and statuary.

Another memento of the Romans: two and a half Corinthian columns, discovered under a nearby street, which have been effectively installed on the edge of a bluff at the end of the **Promenade des Vieilles Murailles** (Old Walls Walk). Spread out below is a neatly gardened park and a port for both pleasure craft and fishing boats.

Rolle. For strategic reasons most medieval castles were built on hilltops, but the 13th-century château of Rolle stands right on the lakefront. It has seen its share of fighting. The Bernese troops who won control of the canton of Vaud in the 16th century burned it twice.

Saint-Prex. In this quaint medieval market town, barns and shops stand among distinguished mansions. A heavy clock tower dated 1234 surmounts the landward side of the short main street leading to the lake.

Morges. When it's tulip time in Morges you know that winter has finally been chased from the lake shore. Every April and May the Morges Tulip Festival features more than 100 varieties of tulips —perhaps 300,000 flowers in all.

Before the railway was built, Morges had been an important port for lake freighters. It's still a nautical centre, but the boats are dinghies and yachts moored in the local marina by weekend sailors who live all along the coast.

Commanding the waterfront, an imposing square Savoyard **château** built in the 13th century now houses an arsenal and the

Vaud Military Museum. In addition to historical costumes, battle flags and weapons, the museum displays legions of toy soldiers. Some 8,000 lead figurines are deployed to recreate ancient and modern battles.

On the main street, the **Musée Alexis Forel** occupies a 16th-century mansion. The collections range from the decorative arts— furniture, porcelain and glass—to dolls, toys and children's games.

Saint-Sulpice. The waterfront park of this quiet village affords striking views of the lake, the mountains and the town of Lausanne, a few kilometres down the coast. Just inland stands an impressive **Romanesque church.** Topped by a heavy square belfry, it was built in the 11th or 12th century as part of a Benedictine priory. In the 15th century the nave collapsed, but the choir and transept still stand.

The setting sun highlights the towers of Lausanne's Gothic cathedral.

Lausanne

Something's always going on in the capital of Vaud—an international music festival, an industrial exhibition or an impromptu street-corner jazz recital. This prosperous lakeside city of 125,000 is headquarters of the

109

International Olympic Committee. Its history goes back to Roman times, when Lousonna, as it was then known, served as an important crossroads town and staging post. By coincidence, the definitive history of Rome was written here. Edward Gibbon (1737–94) finished his *History of the Decline and Fall of the Roman Empire* during the years he spent in Lausanne. Like the empire, Gibbon's house has fallen.

Lausanne's mile-long lakefront of parks, gardens, cafés and restaurants is the liveliest place in town when the weather's fair. More than 1,400 pleasure boats are moored in two local marinas. This part of town, called **Ouchy** (pronounced OO-shee), is also the home port of a veritable Swiss navy of excursion ships. From here lake steamers depart for the French resort towns of Evian (35 minutes) and Thonon.

Take the métro from the lakefront to Place St. François in the city centre, high up the hillside above Ouchy. Fashionable shops line the pedestrian Rue de Bourg. The historic quarter, farther up, surrounds the Gothic **cathedral,** consecrated in 1275. This is one of the last places in the world to preserve the tradition of the night watch. The night hours (10 p.m. to 2 a.m.) are called out by a watchman surveying the city from his tower.

Among 13th-century survivals in this important cathedral are a rare set of choir stalls and a **rose window.** In the fervour of the Reformation almost all the stained-glass windows were shattered, but most of the elements of this admirable squared-circle survived.

Alongside the cathedral, another historic building, the former episcopal palace, is now the **Musée Historique de l'Ancien Evêché.** Archaeological artefacts of the town and the cathedral are on view.

Covered staircases lead from the cathedral to **Place de la Palud,** Lausanne's marketplace since medieval times. On Wednesday and Saturday mornings the entire area becomes an irresistible fruit and vegetable market. This does not detract from the dignity of Lausanne's 17th-century **Hôtel de Ville** (Town Hall), with its arches, clock tower and gargoyles. The fountain in the square bears the figure of Justice.

Lausanne's ten or more museums cover a lot of ground, from the history of the Olympic movement to the history of pipe-smoking. But the **Collection d'Art Brut,** in a converted château near the Beaulieu Palace convention centre, may well be the most original and haunting of Swiss museums. *Art brut* (literally "raw art") is sometimes referred to as "outsiders' art", since it is produced by people living on the periphery of society. The results are astonishing flights of genius by untrained talents, some of them mentally unbalanced. The French artist Jean Dubuffet founded the collection.

The **Maison de l'Hermitage** in north Lausanne offers a gracious setting for excellent temporary art exhibitions. The mansion is situated in full, glorious view of the lake and the old town centre.

Vaud Riviera

From the outskirts of Lausanne to the eastern end of the lake sweeps the Vaud Riviera, known locally as Lavaux, a region of sophisticated resorts and wine-growing villages like Epesses and Saint-Saphorin. No matter how you travel here the views are gripping: by boat looking up at hillsides golden with vines, by train or car right along the coast, by car on the panoramic **Route du Vignoble** or the lofty motorway with its spectacular views.

Wine and chocolate keep the lakeside town of **Vevey** afloat. The biggest building, a modern curved-glass structure, is the world headquarters of Nestlé, the multinational food company. As for wine, the Romans of 2,000 years ago were probably the first to plant the hillsides with grapes.

Vevey's Fête des Vignerons (Winegrowers' Festival), celebrated about once every 25 years since the 16th century, is one of

---

Sweet-Toothed Swiss

The average Swiss, man, woman or child, consumes more than 22 pounds of milk chocolate per year. Logical, you might think, for chocolate is as Swiss as fondue. But it wasn't always so.

Chocolate originated in Mexico. It was brought to Spain by Cortéz in the 16th century, and soon all Europe was drinking it, bitterly. After the Spaniards first produced chocolate in solid form, the Swiss investigated ways of making chocolate taste richer and sweeter. The first chocolate mill in the country was established in Corsier, near Vevey, in the late 18th century.

Among the 19th-century pioneers of the Swiss chocolate industry are names that still sound sweet: Louis-François Cailler, Charles Kohler, Rodolphe Lindt, Henri Nestlé and Philippe Suchard. The difference, of course, is the milk.

Europe's biggest folk manifestations. (The last festival took place in 1977.) A cast of thousands participates in the wine pageant, which occurs in the Grande-Place, Vevey's disproportionately big square. From here extends the attractive old town and the pleasant lakefront promenade.

A cog railway runs from Vevey to **Les Pléiades,** a belvedere 4,474 feet above sea level, with views of the vineyards, the lake and the Alps. About halfway up the hill is **Blonay,** site of a 12th-century château and terminus of a tourist railway equipped with turn-of-the-century locomotives and passenger carriages. Steam's up every weekend from May to the end of October on the Blonay-Chamby line.

From vineyards and orchards above Vevey a funicular climbs to another vantage point, **Mont-Pèlerin,** in a region of woods, farms and villas.

Shielded from north winds at the narrow end of the lake, palmy **Montreux** is a full-time tourist resort, where large old-fashioned hotels and a few new ones cater to

Sailors await a breeze in the small harbour at Lutry, a typical wine-growing town on the Lake of Geneva.

the cosmopolitan visitor's every whim. The service and the view met with the approval of novelist Vladimir Nabokov (father of *Lolita*), who chose to live permanently in a Montreux hotel.

The old-world look of the place is deceptive, for something timely always seems to be going on—an international conference or TV awards or the Montreux Jazz Festival. The casino (the first in Switzerland) on the **waterfront promenade** adds a touch of glamour to the scene, even if confirmed gamblers find it soberly provincial.

Up the hill, away from the glitter of the lakeside is the **old town** with its 18th-century stone houses, chalets, wrought-iron balconies, art galleries, antique and artisans' shops.

In the hothouse micro-climate of Montreux, queen of the Vaud Riviera, all kinds of flowers thrive all year round; even palm trees stand firm on this alien shore. But the town is a springboard for excursions to resorts high above.

A little mountain train goes up to Glion and Caux, a balcony over the lake, and on to **Rochers-de-Naye,** a trip of just under an hour. At 6,700 feet, you'll have an all-encompassing view.

Just east of Montreux lies Switzerland's best-known castle, the **Château of Chillon,** a moody feudal fortress. Its turrets and towers have endured centuries of upheaval and even today they survive the tremor and roar of express trains hurtling past the door.

The great rock of Chillon, projecting from the Lake of Geneva, was always a natural stronghold guarding the highway between Rome and its northern empire. Some fortifications must have been on the spot since ancient times. A rudimentary castle belonging to the bishops of Sion

113

On the Blonay-Chamby line, railway buffs attend to the smallest details.

was greatly strengthened and expanded under the dukes of Savoy. In 1536, after a three-day siege by land and lake, the fortress fell to the Bernese. Nobody welcomed the conquerors to Chillon with more sincere gratitude than François de Bonivard, a Genevan patriot with influential enemies among the Catholic Savoyards. Before his liberation he had spent six years as a prisoner in the château, the final four chained to a pillar.

A couple of centuries later Rousseau wrote briefly about Bo-nivard's suffering. Lord Byron, touring the lake region with Shelley, heard the story in 1816. Generations of school-children, studying Byron's first-person narrative in *The Prisoner of Chillon,* may have thought it was the poet himself locked up inside "Chillon's snow-white battlement". Every year the epic brings several hundred thousand visitors to Chillon.

Apart from the world's most famous dungeon, the château encloses festive banquet halls and flowered courtyards. The alpine views are superb, especially from the prison chamber. Look for Byron's name, inscribed by the poet on one of the pillars.

Four Alpine Resorts

Château-d'Œx (pronounced Château DAY). This appealing family resort is situated in a wide, welcoming valley. An interesting local museum presents the history, arts and crafts of the region. Aerial cableways and ski lifts, plus cross-country trails and year-round hot-air ballooning. In spring the hillsides are white with narcissus instead of snow. Around 35 kilometres from Montreux, the resort is accessible via train, the Montreux-Oberland Bernois line.

Les Diablerets. Chalets are arranged on the hillsides as spontaneously as the dozing cows around this small, family-orien-
tated resort. An aerial cableway goes, in three stages, to the top of Diablerets glacier; year-round high-altitude skiing.

Leysin. On a spectacular, sunny site facing the Dents du Midi and Mont-Blanc, Leysin offers easy and intermediate skiing, as well as sports ranging from ice skating and curling to tennis and archery. The site of a one-time tuberculosis sanitarium, known for its healthy climate.

Villars. Some grand hotels, chalets old and new and apartment blocks in chalet design set the tone for this family resort amid the pines. Very animated on winter weekends. Fairly quiet in summer.

FRIBOURG, NEUCHÂTEL AND JURA

Grouped together here are three areas of western Switzerland, each with its own distinct loyalties and character. The town of Fribourg is the beautiful capital of a region of historic villages and appealing farmlands. Neuchâtel, a university town, borders the largest wholly Swiss lake. And the Jura, rubbing high shoulders with France, is an unspoiled region of rugged cliffs, verdant pastures and pine forests.

Fribourg

The tormented terrain makes Fribourg a three-dimensional town, built both alongside and overhanging its river, the Sarine (*Saane* in German). An unaccountable harmony binds the fine Gothic buildings with the brutally deep gorges and the pastoral scenery beyond.

Founded in 1157 by Duke Berchtold IV of Zähringen, Fribourg joined the Swiss confederation in 1481. When the Protestant Reformation took over its sister city, Berne, Fribourg resisted. And it remains a visibly Catholic town of churches, seminaries and religious bookshops. Even Fribourg's university is Catholic.

It's also a bilingual city, which contributes to its allure. Since the 15th century, when Latin was abandoned as the bureaucratic language, French and German have alternated in power. French finally won out around 1830—but is now losing ground among Fribourg's more than 40,000 citizens.

Sightseeing begins with the dramatic setting of Fribourg: Zähringen Bridge offers the classic scene of the river, the 13th- and 15th-century ramparts on the steep hillside and the old covered bridge linking the banks of the Sarine. There has been a bridge at this point since the 13th century, replaced after every major flood.

Like all the historic buildings of Fribourg, the **Cathédrale Saint-Nicholas** is built of local sandstone, much imperiled by age, weather and the vibration and pollution of traffic. Sad to say, the Gothic statues around the main portal are just copies; the originals had to be moved indoors—to the Catholic University and to the Museum of Art and History. Inside the cathedral, look for the Chapel of the Holy Sepulchre, which contains a moving sculptural ensemble, *The Entombment* (1433).

Another important focus of artistic interest is the Franciscan church, **Eglise des Cordeliers,** founded in the 13th-century. Behind an unremarkable 18th-cen-

Fribourg's dark-green river flows round the red-tiled medieval city.

tury façade lie some outstanding works of art: oak stalls of 1280, the imposing triptych of 1480 over the high altar and the carved and gilded wooden triptych of 1513 in a side chapel.

Just up the street, Fribourg's **Musée d'Art et d'Histoire** occupies the Hôtel Ratzé, a Renaissance mansion that has undergone extensive renovation and expansion. Almost everything on view—from an ornate 2,500-year-old dagger to romantic paintings—originated in Fribourg and vicinity. The town has always been richly supplied with religious art, particularly sculpture, and this is well displayed, starting with a fascinating 10th-century crucifixion scene in stone.

The **Town Hall** *(Hôtel de Ville)* has a steep roof, a covered ceremonial staircase and a turreted

clock tower. Across the square, with its typical fountain, is the sapling of a linden tree—according to tradition, more than 500 years old. When the Swiss defeated Charles the Bold at Morat, it is said, the commander of the Fribourg troops despatched a runner to spread the good news. Arriving at this very spot, the courier cried, "Victory!" with his last breath and died. The story goes that the little branch of linden which decorated the messenger's hat was planted to commemorate the event. Every October thousands of runners retrace the path between Murten and Fribourg in Switzerland's most popular race.

On the way to play at a local festival, a brass band files through farmland.

Around Fribourg

Murten/Morat. This bilingual town is a marvel of perfectly preserved old houses with deep arcades and overhanging roofs. You can climb up to the medieval towers and ramparts to survey the tile roofs, the town's little lake and the countryside. Murten's defences call to mind the battle of June 22, 1476, in which the confederates relieved the besieged town and massacred the army of Charles the Bold.

Although Murten is small, the municipal tourist office issues a map showing all three streets. With or without this assistance, you'll notice the 13th-century château, the solid Berne Gate with its clock and belfry, and the French and German churches. There is also a pleasant museum in a watermill.

In summer, excursion boats cruise the inter-connecting lakes of Murten, Biel and Neuchâtel.

Avenches. Aventicum, as it was called, served as the capital of Roman Helvetia. In about A.D. 260 the dreaded Alemanni tribesmen sacked the town of some 20,000 people, and no one knows what happened to the inhabitants. But overnight Aventicum died. A new town was founded on the same hill in the Middle Ages, but even today the population remains only a fraction of that of the ancient metropolis. At the end of the main street is the **amphi-**theatre which in Roman times seated about 8,000 spectators. It's still a venue for outdoor performances. Just above the main entrance stands a medieval tower, now the nicely organized **Roman Museum.** All the exhibits come from Aventicum.

Payerne. This small Broye Valley town claims Switzerland's greatest Romanesque church, the **Abbatiale,** all that survives of a flourishing Benedictine abbey. After the Reformation the church was abandoned, serving variously as a barn, barracks and prison. But more than 50 years of restoration work has revealed many architectural elements of the 11th century, most strikingly the majestic columns soaring up to the barrel-vaulted roof. In an upstairs chapel you can see a collection of Romanesque stone sculptures of birds, animals and saintly men with troubled faces.

Romont. Thirteenth-century ramparts encircle this market town on a hill midway between Fribourg and Lausanne. You can walk the walls, enjoying a view of the Alps and listening to the soprano bells of the sheep, the contralto bells of the cows and the tenor bells of the church clock tower.

Tourists explore the quaint main street of Gruyères, one of the most picturesque Swiss villages.

The church, an impressive Gothic structure, has medieval and modern stained-glass windows. Romont's fine castle houses a museum devoted to the art of stained glass.

Gruyères. This fortified medieval town situated on top of its own hill attracts sightseers by the coachload. Along the cobbled main street, pipe-smoking farmers in clodhoppers sit on benches staring at tourists taking pictures of the delightful old houses from the 15th to 17th centuries.

The **château,** built by the counts of Gruyères in the Middle Ages, is worth visiting if only for the view from the battlements. The worn steps of the spiral staircase lead to well-preserved state and private apartments. In the castle and the town you'll see the symbol of the counts of Gruyères, a crane *(grue* in French).

Gruyères has come to terms with its situation as one of Switzerland's foremost tourist sights, offering food and drink and all manner of souvenirs to the invading throngs. But cars and tour buses are firmly barred from the town. Industrial manufacture of the renowned cheese of Gruyères is demonstrated in the model factory at the foot of the hill.

The **Musée Gruérien** in the nearby town of Bulle offers interesting insights into the customs and culture of the Gruyères region.

Neuchâtel

The beep-beep-beep of the official Swiss time signal originates at the observatory in Neuchâtel, a centre of scientific research for the watch industry. The university and specialized schools and institutes carry on a long intellectual tradition in this lakeside town of 32,000. Though it's near the frontier between language zones, Neuchâtel claims to speak the purest French in all Switzerland.

Neuchâtel's lake is large enough to accommodate serious regattas and the sizable excursion steamers that cruise northwards and eastwards into the lakes of Biel and Murten. Because it's set on an open plain, the waters can become tempestuous when stormy winds blow.

Strange historical tides have washed across Neuchâtel. It was the possession of the Holy Roman Emperor, the dukes of Burgundy and the kings of Prussia. (Not until the mid-19th century did Prussia go through the formalities of setting Neuchâtel free—more than 40 years after it had joined the Swiss confederation.)

The old crossroads of the town, Croix-du-Marché, is only a few streets inland from the compact port of Neuchâtel. Among buildings and fountains dating from the 16th to the 18th centuries, the most original construction is

The outdoor café habit is deeply ingrained in Switzerland, happily.

Maison des Halles (1575), designed as a covered market.

At the top of the town is a monumental medieval complex that neatly blurred the line dividing church and state. Church, prison and government headquarters all stood together behind common defences. Inside the great Romanesque-Gothic church, the **Collégiale,** a remarkable sculptural group immortalizes the counts of Neuchâtel. There are 15 polychrome figures, all life size.

The château, built between the 12th and 16th centuries, now serves as the seat of the cantonal government. The best vantage point over the town and the lake is the top of the 15th-century prison tower… if you don't mind walking up 125 wooden steps.

Further on, in the **Musée d'Eth-nographie,** you can see fine and extremely well-presented collections from ancient Egypt, Africa and Oceania.

Neuchâtel's two most important museums share a building at the port. The **Musée des Beaux-Arts** exhibits Swiss artists and medieval religious paintings, while the **Musée d'Histoire** exhibits rare Swiss ceramics, 16th-century pocket watches, assorted armour, coins and medals. Best of all are three androids—robots in human form—made by the 18th-century Swiss clockmakers Pierre and Henri-Louis Jaquet-Droz, a father and son. Called the *Musician,* the *Draughtsman* and the *Writer,* they move with seemingly human grace. On the first Sunday of each month from 2.30 to 4 p.m. the automatons give a command performance.

Around the Lake of Neuchâtel

Grandson. This picturesque town of 2,000 inhabitants was the scene of a famous triumph in Swiss history. Confederate troops from Berne and central Switzerland defeated Charles the Bold, Duke of Burgundy, here in 1476. For a vivid reconstruction of the event, see the deployment of toy soldiers in Grandson's five-towered châ-

teau. You can explore the ramparts of the castle, built in the 13th century, and admire Greta Garbo's 1923 Rolls Royce in the antique car museum.

Yverdon-les-Bains. Known for its mineral baths since Roman times, this spa is flourishing again. You can bathe in what is called the biggest outdoor thermal pool in Switzerland. A 13th-century castle in the centre

of town houses the municipal museum, an eclectic collection that covers a lot of ground, from caveman relics to primitive bicycles, with a couple of Egyptian mummies for good measure.

Estavayer-le-Lac. All manner of architecture stands side by side in this old walled town. The 13th-century Château de Chenaux, headquarters for the local police force, once belonged to the dukes of Savoy. The church in the centre of town *(St. Laurent)* is mostly late Gothic.

The Jura

Somewhat removed from the main tourist routes, the Jura concentrates a strong local pride, now wrapped in the flag of the new Jura canton, created in 1979. Life can be harsh in this sparsely settled border region, where watchmaking has been a vital cottage industry for centuries. The Jura scatters its charms through the high limestone ridges and valleys that extend from south-west to north-east, from the outskirts of Geneva almost to Basle, encompassing half a dozen cantons, including that of Jura.

Romainmôtier. This charming village, set in an idyllic little val-

Horses and cows share rich grass off the tourist track in the Jura.

ley, takes its name from the monastery (*moutier* in Old French) established here around the year 450 by St. Romain. The present **church,** the third on the site, was built in the 10th and 11th centuries. Influenced by French architecture of the time, Romainmôtier has a majesty all its own.

The outlines of the earlier churches are still visible in the floor near the organ. Look for the 12th- and 13th-century frescoes and the Romanesque sculptures of medieval horrors and marvels. The rarest piece of carved stone is the 7th-century ambo, an early Christian pulpit.

Of the monastery buildings, a 14th-century clock tower and a 15th-century prior's house remain.

La Chaux-de-Fonds. In La Chaux-de-Fonds more than most

places, time is money. The industrial base for this town of nearly 40,000 inhabitants is watchmaking. **The Musée International d'Horlogerie**—one of the best designed museums in Switzerland—runs the gamut from sundials and sand clocks to the most modern chronometers. A highlight of the 3,000-piece collection are some rare enamelled pieces of the 17th-century. You can observe artisans restoring antique clocks and watches and learn about the latest Swiss efforts to keep ahead of the competition in technology.

North of town begin the forests and pastureland of the **Franches-Montagnes,** a high mountain plateau that extends as far as Saint-Ursanne. Horse breeding is the principal activity of this peaceful, pastoral region, a centre for riding, hiking and cross-country skiing.

Saint-Ursanne. Situated on a bend in the rushing River Doubs, St. Ursanne is as charming a hamlet as you'll ever see. Pink, ochre and white stone houses, some of them tottering with age, crowd against the river bank. Under the arched, one-lane bridge, kingfishers dart above the water. Old men in black berets bask in the sunshine alongside the impos-

Relics in the Jura: a vintage clock and a venerable religious sculpture.

ing **collegiate church,** noted for its Romanesque south portal. Like the village, the church is named after St. Ursicinus, a wandering Irishman of the 7th century, who lived as a hermit alongside the River Doubs.

Porrentruy. Halfway between La Chaux-de-Fonds and Basle, the Swiss border makes an arrow-shaped incursion into France. At the centre of this hilly "peninsula" is Porrentruy, a town with a distinguished history. In 1527, when the Reformation was established in Basle, the prince-bishop retreated to Porrentruy.

For two-and-a-half centuries this small Jura town was a considerable religious and political capital, and many of the buildings attest to its former stature.

The prince-bishop installed himself in the medieval **château** and proceeded to extend it, constructing a residence and administrative headquarters. The 16th-century tower still sports the episcopal shield. The Town Hall and other 18th-century buildings in the French style symbolize close ties with France, just across the border. As a matter of fact, France annexed the town for a time, after the Revolution. Wrought-iron balconies and shuttered windows of unexpected sizes and shapes make Porrentruy look more French than Swiss and more princely than most towns of 7,000 souls.

GENEVA

Diplomats and international functionaries hang on tenaciously when threatened with a transfer from this gracious city of history and the arts, elegant shops and restaurants and waterfront parks. After all, Geneva (*Genève* in French, *Genf* in German) has that lake, those mountains, that mild climate.

Geneva's situation has been considered crucial ever since 58 B.C., when Julius Caesar and his legions arrived on the scene. They destroyed the ancient bridge across the Rhone to bar Helvetian tribesmen from migrating to the colony of Gaul. Many another ruler has coveted Geneva and its strategic traffic and trade. The city has been variously controlled by the kings of Burgundy, the Holy Roman Emperor, the dukes of Savoy and, briefly, Napoleon Bonaparte.

In the most memorable battle for Geneva, several thousand mercenaries under the Savoyard flag attacked in 1602. They scaled the town wall at night, but the citizens, armed with everything from pikes to stewpots, sent them flying. Every December 11, Geneva celebrates Escalade (Scaling of the Walls) with a triumphant torchlight parade.

Perhaps the most improbable ruler in the town's history, the French theologian John Calvin, made Geneva a great Protestant centre. In 1541, the citizens invited him to serve as their spiritual leader. Protestant refugees and pilgrims poured into the town, but Calvinist rule proved dour and unbending. Today tolerance reigns. Geneva, headquarters of the World Council of Churches, is well supplied with Protestant, Catholic and Orthodox churches, plus a synagogue and a mosque.

Walking through Geneva

A pedestrian precinct leads from the railway station, Gare Cornavin, towards the lakeside. It's only a five-minute walk, if you can stay aloof from the shops and cafés along the way.

The tallest monument in Geneva, visible from many parts of town, is as impermanent as a summer shower. It is, in fact, a jet of water prosaically named the **Jet d'Eau.** When the wind is still, the pump sprays lake water straight up to the height of a 40-storey building. A fountain has been the trademark of Geneva's harbour for nearly a century, though the modern model is far more powerful—and more expensive to run.

The Mont-Blanc bridge is the longest and busiest link between the two halves of Geneva. Here you can sense a drastic change in the waterway, which narrows to become a surging river. The Rhone, born high in the Alps, flows the length of the Lake of Geneva until this spot, where the lake ends and the mighty river resumes its rush towards the Mediterranean. From the head of the bridge, on the right bank, you have a perfect view of Mont-Blanc itself, across the border in the French Alps.

Notice the small wooded island (man-made in the 16th century) just west of the Mont-Blanc bridge. The contemplative statue honours a distinguished Genevan, the philosopher Jean-Jacques Rousseau (1712–78). A larger island, down-river, bears the laconic name of **l'Ile** (The Island). The tower here is all that remains of a château constructed in 1219; a plaque cites a quotation from Caesar.

Once across the river you can make for Geneva's elegant **shopping district,** centred on Rue du Rhone and the two parallel streets beyond, or wander up Rue de la Corraterie, another smart shopping street, to Place Neuve. Presiding over the square are three Geneva landmarks: the **Grand Théâtre** (a smaller version of the Paris opera house), the Conservatoire de Musique, and the **Musée Rath,** which presents temporary art exhibitions.

Behind the iron gates of Promenade des Bastions, the park facing Place Neuve, stands the imposing **Reformation Monument.** A long stone wall is engraved with religious texts in several languages

129

Fine ensemble of low-rise buildings graces the right bank of Geneva.

(including 16th-century English). The central sculptural group portrays Calvin and three of his associates: the French reformers Théodore de Bèze and Guillaume Farel, and the Scottish preacher John Knox. Opposite the monument is the main building of the University of Geneva, a descendant of Calvin's theological academy.

Uphill from here is Geneva's **old town,** a well-preserved quarter of twisting cobbled streets and historic mansions. Because of the strategic hilltop location, this was the area first fortified by the Romans; you'll see restored portions of the ancient city walls.

If you go up via Rue St-Léger, at the far side of Promenade des Bastions, you'll arrive at **Place du Bourg-de-Four,** site of the old Roman forum. Fronting on the square are the Palais de Justice (1712) and houses of the 16th to 18th centuries. Turn into Rue de l'Hôtel-de-Ville, lined with some of Geneva's most prestigious antique shops, and continue to Place de la Taconnerie. Here you can visit the modest chapel in which John Knox preached to English-language adherents of the new faith. A few steps away is Geneva's cathedral.

The highest point of the old town has been a place of worship since pagan days. The present **Cathédrale St-Pierre** (St. Peter's Cathedral) was begun in the 12th century in Romanesque style but evolved into Gothic innovation. In the 18th century the façade was remodelled, and classical columns, still controversial, were added.

The interior has been restored. It is as austere as the doctrine of Calvin, who preached here for more than 20 years. The Flamboyant Gothic Chapel of the Maccabees can be reached by a separate entrance on the south side. From the top of the north tower, amid the carillon bells, there's a top-flight **panorama** of Geneva and vicinity.

Geneva's oldest surviving house, Maison Tavel, lies nearby in Rue du Puits-St. Pierre. Further along, at the crossing of Rue de l'Hôtel-de-Ville, you come to a building called the **Arsenal,** the former granary. In the arcades, partly camouflaged by flower pots, cannon from the 17th and 18th centuries are symbolically deployed. Modern mosaics give an impression of medieval Geneva.

Across the street from the Arsenal, Geneva's **Hôtel de Ville** (Town Hall) has a harmonious Renaissance courtyard, a venue for concerts in summer. The first of the Geneva conventions on the

131

humane treatment of prisoners-of-war was concluded in the Town Hall in 1864. Soon afterwards, an international dispute growing out of the American Civil War was settled here. The historic chamber is now called, somewhat startlingly, the Salle de l'Alabama—after a Confederate warship of the same name.

Behind the Town Hall, on a bluff overlooking Promenade des Bastions, you can relax in a tree-shaded park called La Treille (The Trellis).

The street running past the Town Hall turns into the picturesque **Grand-Rue,** built with houses from the 15th to 18th centuries. A plaque on the front of No. 40 indicates the birthplace of Jean-Jacques Rousseau. Houses in Louis XVI style line the parallel **Rue des Granges.**

International City

The elegant Quai Wilson, along the right bank of the lake, honours the 20th-century American president who profoundly affected Geneva's destiny. The city had long been a centre of banking and watch-making, as well as intellectual and humanitarian activities when Woodrow Wilson made it the world headquarters of diplomacy. Founding the League of Nations in 1920, he nominated Geneva as its site.

In the decades since that momentous event, countless new international organizations and agencies have established headquarters in the congenial surroundings of Geneva. They are as diverse as the International Telecommunications Union, the International Labour Office (ILO), the General Agreement of Tariffs and Trade (GATT) and the World Organization for the Protection of Intellectual Property.

The vast **Palais des Nations** opened as headquarters of the League of Nations in 1937, when war clouds already overshadowed the League's attempts to achieve international cooperation. After World War II, the new United Nations took over the building for its European headquarters. As U.N. activities and personnel rolls inexorably multiplied, the building was further expanded, rapidly eclipsing the Palace of Versailles in area. The U.N. runs guided tours of the historic conference rooms.

Parks and Gardens

Geneva is rightly proud of its spacious parks with their fountains, sculptures, bandstands and cafés. Most of the parks were private tracts of land bequeathed to the city. The highlights:

Jardin Anglais (English Garden), on the left bank, is best known for its flower clock—a huge dial made up of thousands of flowers and plants changed seasonally. **Parc de La Grange** features a rose garden that blooms extravagantly in June; **Parc des Eaux Vives,** adjoining, is beautifully landscaped.

On the right bank, in **Jardin Brunswick** on the Quai du Mont-Blanc stands Geneva's most pompous monument: the tomb of the Duke of Brunswick (1804–73). The duke, who spent his last few years in exile in Geneva, left all his money to the city, with the proviso that a mausoleum be erected in his honour.

Stroll through the lakeside parks of **Mon-Repos** and **Perle du Lac** to reach Geneva's **Botanical Garden** *(Jardin Botanique)*. The adjacent Parc de l'Ariana surrounds the U.N.

Bric-a-brac and paintings of alpine scenes on sale at a Geneva shop.

Museums of Geneva

Musée d'Art et d'Histoire (Rue Charles Galland). Chiefly a collection of archaeology, fine and decorative arts. The fine arts section concentrates on the Dutch, Flemish, French and Swiss masters. The most prized exhibit is an altarpiece of 1444, painted by Konrad Witz for Geneva's cathedral. Titled *La Pêche Miraculeuse* (The Miraculous Draught of Fishes), it is the first painting in the history of European art to depict an identifiable landscape. Christ is shown walking on the water of Geneva's lake, while in the distance rises Mt. Salève.

Musée de l'Horlogerie et de l'Emaillerie (15, Route de Malagnou). An 18th-century mansion houses the collection of clocks, watches and enamelwork spanning the centuries from the Renaissance to the present day. The emphasis is on lesser-known artists.

Petit Palais (2 terrace Saint-Victor). Four floors of this small palace are filled with Impressionist and post-Impressionist works of varying quality.

Geneva has about a dozen more museums, including a pair devoted to the men who made the city a great intellectual centre in the 18th-century—Rousseau and Voltaire. In spite of their vastly differing views and styles, both authors at one time had their works banned by Geneva's ultra-righteous censor.

Carouge

Although it seems like an extension of Geneva, Carouge is a separate municipality on the south bank of the River Arve with its own history and character. It was founded in the late 18th century by the King of Sardinia, who also happened to be Duke of Savoy. His imperial plan involved the creation of a city to rival Geneva. Most of the architecture projected for Carouge remained on the drawing board, but there's no mistaking the Mediterranean charm of the town's fountains and squares, wrought-iron street lamps and faded town houses.

Genevans go to Carouge for a touch of bohemia—for theatre, art events, lively bars and restaurants. A colourful street market is held on Wednesday and Saturday.

Foreign Affairs

Geneva is surrounded on three sides by the Savoy region of France, so crossing the border is as commonplace as crossing town. Here are two detours across the nearby frontier.

The Salève. This mountain is such a familiar bit of scenery for Genevans that it might as well be a local monument. On weekends the strangely tilted cliff-face attracts local mountain climbers. Other intrepid sportsmen drive to the top (4,525 feet) to practise the breathtaking art of hang-gliding.

Take the cable car to the summit. The view is superb.

Divonne. In this overgrown French village, 18 kilometres north of Geneva, you can restore your health or (much less likely) your fortune. The two principal attractions are the thermal baths and the gambling casino—one of the busiest in all France. Big money changes hands around the roulette, blackjack, baccarat and dice tables in an old-fashioned continental atmosphere. In summer Divonne widens its horizons with horse-racing, golf, sailing and a distinguished festival of chamber music.

An Ill Wind or Two

The Swiss worry about their wind currents the way the French worry about their livers. If the wind blows from the north-east, a cold bise, it's the subject of knowing conversation all day. If it's a dry, warm föhn, they say, you can experience headaches, fatigue and sometimes vertigo. One Swiss company markets pocket-sized magnetic field generators expressly to ease the unpleasant effects of this particular wind.

Down at the lakes, charts warn sailors to watch for legendary local winds that blow no good. On Lac Léman the most tempestuous of all, the bornan originates in France and comes on at a hurricane-like intensity.

WHAT TO DO

Switzerland has a great deal to offer: folklore and festivals, elegant shopping, history and art and music. Or nothing more strenuous than a stroll in unadulterated mountain air.

Sports

Sports top the charts for active holidaymakers in Switzerland, where almost every interest can be satisfied, from skiing to mountain-climbing and golf to horse-riding. Though its winter sports facilities are best known, the country stays uncommonly sports-minded in all seasons.

Skiing

Experts and amateurs alike pronounce Switzerland the summit of skiing, the home of exhilarating sport in optimum conditions of comfort, safety and sheer natural beauty.

Nearly 200 Swiss towns and villages are geared for downhill skiing, among them famous resorts like St. Moritz, Zermatt and Gstaad. In most areas the season runs from late November to early April, but conditions vary from year to year and resort to resort. The Christmas and Easter holiday periods are high season for prices and crowds, when you have to reach the lifts early in the morning to avoid long queues. Outside these popular times, a variety of money-saving package tours are on offer, including hotel, meals and ski instruction. Throughout the winter season, the Swiss Ski School organizes excellent group classes and provides highly qualified teachers for private individuals. The tourist office has full details.

Skiers should take special care to avoid sunburn and snow-blindness. The altitude itself can be debilitating, so don't overdo it until you adjust. Statistics show that most skiers who are injured succumb either on the first or last day of their holiday—in the first case due to lack of preparation, and in the latter because, over-confident, they were eager to squeeze in one final thrill. But if the worst should happen, be assured that the safety patrols—including a helicopter rescue service—know how to handle any emergency.

Cross-country skiing (*Langlauf* in German, *ski de fond* in French) has seen a great surge in popularity in recent years. Strike out through forested country or follow the course of an alpine stream. Stop along the way for a winter picnic or eat at an open-air restaurant. All runs are signposted according to difficulty. Some resorts have 60 miles or more of trails, and new ones open up every season.

Other Winter Sports

Ski-bobbing, rather like bicycling on snow, offers plenty of down-to-earth thrills. Ski-bobs can be rented at resorts, some of which reserve special slopes.

Ice-skating. Most ski resorts have natural ice rinks in a winter wonderland setting; some have artificial rinks as well. Skates and lessons are available on the spot.

Curling. This gentlemanly sport, as inscrutable as ice-fishing, is practiced in many resorts. Play proceeds in slow motion, as competitors coax heavy granite

High spirits and sunny ski trails add to the popularity of Swiss resorts.

curling stones across the ice, either in the open or in more comfortable covered ice-rinks.

Summer Sports

High-altitude resorts like Les Diablerets, Verbier, Zermatt, Saas-Fee and Pontresina take advantage of the eternal snows to offer **summer skiing** for those who can't wait until next season. It's quite common for holidaymakers to ski in the morning and swim in the afternoon. Many resorts keep aerial cableways and ski lifts running in summer for the benefit of hikers and mountain-climbers, as well as sedentary sightseers.

Mountain climbing. Expert guidance and proper equipment are vital for any ascent. Rescue teams sometimes find that accident victims are dressed for a tennis match instead of a challenging encounter with nature at its trickiest. The only sane course for the inexperienced is to enroll in a mountain-climbing school.

Mountain trekking is another matter. Just don't stray from the marked paths, which go up to about 8,000 feet—and wear sensible boots. Arm yourself with the detailed maps prepared by the Federal Topographic Survey. Invaluable, too, is the list of mountain huts available from the Swiss Alpine Club.

Hiking. Switzerland offers around 30,000 miles of signposted footpaths. Everywhere you wander you'll see the yellow signs that mark the trails and tell you how long it will take to reach your destination. Various books, leaflets and maps are available suggesting rambles through the most attractive countryside. Many resorts organize conducted walking and climbing tours. For further information, consult the fact sheet entitled "Hiking in Switzerland", available from the tourist office.

Swimming. Water temperatures in the mountain lakes may seem chilly to visitors accustomed to the Gulf Stream, but most towns have heated public pools (often indoors) equipped with changing rooms and showers.

Boating. Every summer weekend somewhere in Switzerland there's a major regatta. On most of the Swiss lakes, you can hire a boat—or a pedalo—though you need a license to captain a vessel with more than 150 square feet of sail. Rowing and canoeing are popular, too. Winds on the lakes can be exceedingly unpredictable because of the surrounding mountains.

Water-skiing. This expensive sport can be pursued in most major resorts, though it may be barred in some places because of restrictions on speedboats.

Board-sailing (windsurfing). You can hire equipment and arrange for lessons in the popular resorts.

Fishing. Lakes and mountain streams are stocked annually with trout, grayling and pike. Local police stations issue fishing licenses by the day, week or month. Inquire on the spot about restrictions and regulations, as these vary from place to place.

Racers round the buoy in a regatta on Silvaplana Lake, in Engadine.

Golf. All told, there are some 30 courses in Switzerland. In the Alps, any place big enough to be called a plateau probably has a golf course—but the magnificent scenery may just distract you from your game. Normally members of golf clubs in their home countries can play Swiss courses for a greens fee.

Tennis. Most resorts have courts, as do the principal towns

—though municipal facilities are often crowded. Lessons can usually be arranged. The Swiss International Tennis Championships in Gstaad attract top players every summer.

Riding. Stables, riding schools and equestrian centres may be found near cities and in resort areas. Some resorts organize cross-country riding holidays. Ask the tourist office for details.

Cycling. You can rent a bike at any railway station and turn it in at another further along the line whenever you get tired. But don't forget there's a lot of uphill pedalling. The tourist office distributes a helpful booklet, *Bicycling in Switzerland*.

Festivals and Folklore

It might not be as riotous as carnival in Basle or as decorous as tulip time in Morges, but you'll probably come across a festival at some point in your Swiss travels. No village is so small that it doesn't stage some sort of local festivity at least once a year. The Swiss National Tourist Office publishes a booklet entitled *Events in Switzerland*, listing everything from jazz concerts and ballet to alpine herdsmen's festivals for the year ahead. Or you can ask your hotel receptionist if any fêtes are scheduled in the area.

Folklore manifestations complete with traditional dancing and country songs turn up everywhere. You may even hear the alphorn, a bizarre wind instrument twice as long as a man is tall. Yodelling may be encountered in certain restaurants in German-speaking Switzerland as well as at festivals.

Swiss wrestling (*"Hosenlupf"* or *lutte suisse*) is a rare sport with roots far back in history. The gladiators, dressed in special short trousers, struggle fiercely to throw each other on the sawdust while holding to strict rules of chivalry.

Colourful Valais cowfights (cow versus cow) may be seen in one valley or another on Sundays in springtime.

Here are some events from a typical year's calendar:

January. Folk celebrations in towns and villages usher in the New Year. Horse-racing on snow in St. Moritz and Arosa. Vogel-Gryff Day in Basle.

February/March. Carnival processions in Basle, Lucerne and lesser-known Fasnacht centres.

March. Chalanda Marz processions, of pagan origin, in the Engadine. Thousands of contestants join the Engadine cross-country ski marathon.

April. Zurich parade and bonfire to welcome spring.

Between vineyards and green fields, cyclists savour the Swiss countryside.

WHAT TO DO

April/May. Landsgemeinde in Appenzell and some other cantons.

June. Celebrations accompany the cows to alpine pastures. Zurich's International June Festival features concerts, opera, theatre and art exhibitions. International Little Theatres Festival in Berne.

July. Montreux Jazz Festival. Nyon Folk Music Festival.

August. National Day celebrations. Music festivals in Lucerne and Gstaad. Locarno International Film Festival. Fireworks and parades of Fête de Genève.

September. Music festivals in Montreux and Vevey.

September/October. Vintage festivals in vineyard regions.

November. Onion market, of medieval tradition, in Berne.

December. Torchlight Escalade procession in Geneva.

Shopping

Cheese, chocolate and clocks are the obvious purchases. But the frontiers of shopping in Switzerland are much more expansive. And, alas, expensive.

Some of the best buys are in the luxury range—furs, watches and jewellery are all competitively priced. Conversely, the price tags on many mass-market items prove discouragingly high for visitors from most countries, owing to the solidity of the Swiss franc. Even so, you're sure of the best quality; the Swiss themselves may well be the world's most demanding customers. Sales personnel are usually extremely helpful and polite and really know their merchandise.

Bargains, if any, are to be discovered during sales in January/February and July/August. Switzerland has no sales tax or VAT—the price you see is the one you pay.

Where to Shop

Zurich and Geneva are international capitals of elegant shopping, with especially good browsing in Lucerne, Basle and Berne, as well as in resorts like Gstaad or St. Moritz. The budget-minded should check out the supermarket chain stores.

Down to earth: traditional wrestlers and impeccably arrayed vegetables.

What to Buy

Antiques. If you're in the market for an Empire clock or a piece of Nyon porcelain, Switzerland's dealers may have just the thing for you. Rustic furniture and old farm implements feature in the show windows of many shops. Fine jewels, old silver and other items are offered for sale at the periodic auctions held in Zurich and Geneva. At the other end of the market, collectibles (and plenty of irresistible junk) turn up at big city street markets and local fairs.

Art. Galleries abound in Zurich, Basle, Geneva, Lausanne and many smaller towns. Experts point out that the prices for fine art are no higher in Switzerland than anywhere else, especially when it comes to avant-garde work. Dealers are accustomed to shipping paintings and sculpture to the ends of the earth.

Brandies. Potent and portable, Swiss spirits make a long-lasting souvenir or gift. They're made from apples, cherries, grapes, pears, plums and Alpine herbs.

Cheese. Some Swiss cheeses travel well; ask in any cheese shop for advice.

Chocolate. From supermarket bars to hand-dipped truffles Switzerland produces what must be the world's largest variety of chocolate confections.

Clocks. Department stores and souvenir shops carry cuckoo clocks in all sizes and styles. You probably won't find a "Made in Switzerland" label, since most of them come from Germany.

If bird imitations are too frivolous for your taste, think about a sober Swiss alarm clock—or an 18th-century-style pendulum.

Embroidery. Hand towels and table cloths, shirts and blouses are decorated with the stitching of St. Gall.

Footwear. The Swiss manufacture everything from high fashion shoes to sturdy hiking boots that can stand up to the toughest mountain trek.

Jewellery. Articles of gold and stones of impeccable quality are offered for sale. Look over the glamorous displays in principal shopping streets, but don't forget the small merchants with premises hidden away in old town neighbourhoods.

Knives. The Swiss Army invention—essentially a pocket tool kit—reveals as many as 13 gadgets from a corkscrew to a miniature saw.

Masks. Search out examples of this old folk art from mountain villages of the Lötschental or from the town of Brienz.

Pottery. A traditional Swiss speciality, with interesting regional variations.

Art and commerce converge in the show window of a Geneva shop.

Souvenirs. Alpenstocks, cowbells, dolls in regional costumes, recordings of yodelling music. Kitsch aside, look for alpine fossils and minerals or the hand-crafted articles available from the Heimatwerk shops: wooden toys, bowls and plates, music boxes, copper pots, pewter glass, painted Easter eggs.

Watches. Reliable shops everywhere stock all the famous makes, so it's just a matter of tracking down the style or price that suits you. Be sure your new timepiece comes with an international guarantee.

Entertainment

Considering that Swiss cities are really small towns by the standards of London or New York, the after-dark scene is livelier than might be expected. Even in relatively isolated places you'll probably find a disco or a dance, a convivial café or a concert. Still, "swinging" is not quite the label for Switzerland, a country where people have to show up at work as early as 7 o'clock the morning after.

For uninhibited nightlife you have to go to the big ski resorts. Here all conditions conspire to enliven the recreation-by-moonlight—the altitude, fresh air, sense of physical well-being, absence of routine cares and a contagious *joie de vivre*. The music blares far into the night as ski-strained muscles work overtime on the dance floor.

Nightclubs with floor shows, bands, even professional dancing partners may be found in big towns like Zurich and Geneva, John Calvin's bastion of morality. Elsewhere, entertainment may consist of nothing more elaborate than a local folklore group or a pianist. But what more could one want while nursing a roaring fire in a mountain lodge? Or, on a fine summer night, you can board one of the lake steamers shanghaied for a dancing cruise. The romantic ingredients are convincing—the music, the lake, the stars, the Alps....

Swiss towns large and small figure on the international classical concert circuit and prominent artists appear frequently. Local chamber groups and symphony orchestras like the renowned Orchestre de la Suisse Romande often give performances on their home turf. What could be more effective than medieval music in the courtyard of a château or an organ recital in a historic church? Many Swiss cities organize annual music festivals; the most prestigious is held every summer in Lucerne.

Opera and ballet featuring guest stars and local talent alike is an important part of the scene in Zurich, Geneva, Basle, Berne, and smaller towns.

Jazz, traditional and avant-garde, is not neglected. The regional concerts given throughout the year are just a warm-up for the summer's summit meeting at the Montreux Festival.

Theatre can be lively in the big centres, but you have to know the language—German in Zurich, Basle and Berne, French in Geneva and Lausanne.

In resort and metropolitan areas some cinemas show films in the original language with subtitles in French and German. Otherwise, the soundtrack is dubbed into the language of the region. Locarno's film festival is internationally renowned.

EATING OUT

There's more to Swiss cuisine than *fondue*. But, like that inspired cheese concoction, most dishes tend to be very filling. The portions are gargantuan, and many restaurants serve second helpings on a clean plate as big as the first. Just keep your knife and fork… and your determination to struggle on.

Each region has its specialities, often influenced by the traditions of the neighbouring country that shares its language.

Taking a break from the pressures of the Montreux Jazz Festival.

Fondue and Cheeses

More than a meal, cheese *fondue* is a social occasion. The celebrants gather around a bubbling cauldron containing a mixture of cheeses diluted with white wine and a dash of cherry brandy. With special long forks they dip chunks of bread in the melted cheese.

Fondue bourguignonne. This time the pot is filled with boiling oil, into which the diners dip pieces of meat. After each bit is cooked, flavour it with one of the sauces provided.

Fondue chinoise, the "Chinese" version. Now thinly sliced meat is plunged into simmering stock. The rich broth is served to finish.

Raclette. Half a big wheel of cheese is brought close to a heating element—or more authentically, the flame of a wood fire. As it begins to melt, the cook scrapes off a portion—crispy rind and all—onto your plate. Eaten with boiled potatoes (peel them yourself), pickled onions and gherkins. (Note: Only white wine or hot tea should be drunk with *fondue* or *raclette;* cold drinks imbibed during or immediately after these meals cause digestive distress.)

Swiss cheeses. Although few Swiss restaurants serve a cheese course in the French style, you may be tempted to visit a cheese shop or the market and pick up the makings of a picnic.

Emmentaler is the mild cheese with holes known in some other countries as "Swiss cheese". *Appenzeller* tastes tangier; *Gruyère* (*Greyerzer* in German), usually more salty, has a nutty flavour. *Sbrinz* resembles Parmesan. *Vacherin,* an unctuous, runny cheese, is available only in winter. Hard, round and pungent, *Tête de moine* does indeed look like the head of a bald monk. *Tomme vaudoise,* a flat, mild, soft cheese, sometimes contains caraway seeds. *Reblochon,* a soft, creamy, delicious white cheese, may be a bit on the pungent side.

For a cheesy snack, try a hot cheese tart—*Käsewähe* or *ramequin*—or a *Käseschnitte* or *croûte au fromage,* an open-faced melted cheese sandwich.

Swiss-German Specialities

Soups. Long, cold winters inspire an enormous variety of appetizing soups. Among them: *Basler Mehlsuppe* (Basle flour soup), eaten in the wee hours during the city's carnival, and *Brotsuppe* (bread soup), a favourite of Lucerne.

Fish. Look for *Felchen,* a kind of trout, caught in all the Swiss lakes; freshwater *Egli* (perch); *Forellen* (trout), often commercially bred; and the related, red-

On a cold winter day, a hot grill attracts a flock of hungry skiers.

tinted *Rötel* from the Lake of Zug and the river fish *Aesche,* both found only in late autumn and winter.

Meat. Zurich's nationally-esteemed speciality is *Geschnetzeltes Kalbfleisch* (diced veal in a rich cream sauce), known in the French-speaking sector as *Emincé zurichoise.* Another dish linked to a specific region is *Bernerplatte* (Bernese board), laden with a variety of meats, sausage, sauerkraut or dried French beans and potatoes. A speciality of the Grisons, *Bündnerfleisch* (paper-thin slices of air-dried beef) is a favourite savoury snack and starter.

Game. Served during the September-to-February hunting season, venison, deer, wild boar and hare dishes are much appreciated. *Rehrücken* (saddle of venison) is roasted and served with red cabbage and a cream sauce.

Sausages. Switzerland produces an extraordinary variety—at least 45 different types. Eat Swiss sausages boiled, fried, grilled or cold. Sausage specialities include *Schübling,* pork sausage, *Bratwurst mit Zwiebelsauce,* veal sausage with onion sauce, and *Cervelatsalat,* sausage salad.

Potatoes and Noodles. Don't leave Switzerland without trying *Rösti,* potatoes fried with onion. Another companion to meat (especially game) dishes: *Spätzli,* tiny, noodle-like dumplings.

Swiss-French Specialities

Fish. *Omble chevalier* (char) has been hailed as the most delicate and flavourful of all freshwater fish; it's usually poached and served with hollandaise. Otherwise, look for lake trout *(truite)* or salmon trout *(truite saumonée),* a tender cousin with slightly pink flesh. *Perche* (perch) is usually filleted, fried and served with a slice of lemon and tartar sauce. *Brochet* (pike) may be grilled or incorporated in dumplings and bathed in a white-wine sauce *(quenelles de brochet),* while *féra,* a kind of lake trout, is baked or sautéed.

Meat. The French influence is evident in the steaks—*entrecôte* (boned sirloin or rib-eye steak) and *tournedos* (fillet steak). From the Valais comes *Assiette Valaisanne,* thin slices of dried beef, cured ham, dried bacon, sausages, cheese and gherkins. The invariable accompaniment is *pain de seigle,* rich dark rye bread.

Swiss-Italian Specialities

In the Ticino, dishes and recipes are Italian—*piccata, saltimbocca, osso bucco.* You can dine on pasta or pizza, but a more typical Ticino dish is *risotto,* a rich rice invention flavoured with onion, mushroom and, finally, a sprinkling of grated cheese.

One big favourite as an accompaniment to meat dishes is *polenta,* a sort of maize porridge; an authentic local restaurant is likely to have a big cauldron of polenta on the fire. When made with cream in the Ticino style, it is called *polenta grassa*.

Desserts

Swiss fruit tarts are eaten as sweets or snacks and, in some circles, as a meal in itself. *Zuger Kirschtorte* is an enticing cherry-brandy cake from Zug. *Rüeblitorte* features carrots with eggs, almonds, cinnamon and brandy.

In season the fresh fruit can be good. Or see if you're equal to one of those towering Swiss ice-cream sundaes.

Swiss Wines

In a bar or restaurant wine is ordered by the bottle or half-bottle, or by the carafe in multiples of one decilitre (one-tenth of a litre). Many Swiss wines are named after the grape used. In some establishments you can further specify the region whose wine you want. A list is always displayed in cafés and *pintes*. Note that the Swiss normally drink white wine with fondue, raclette and other cheese preparations.

The Valais, Vaud and Geneva are the biggest wine-producing regions in Switzerland. Most common and best by far are white wines—the fruity *Fendant* and the slightly stronger *Johannisberg*. Swiss white wines have a distinctive, slightly acid taste, often

faintly fizzy with a flinty quality. As for the reds, try the full-flavoured *Dôle* or *Pinot Noir*.

While the wine of German-speaking Switzerland has less renown, you may want to try some of the light, dry reds *(Hallauer, Maienfelder, Klevner, Stammheimer)*. The wine generally found in the Ticino is *Merlot,* a sturdy ruby red.

Other Drinks

Swiss lager is sold under various brand names in bottles and on tap. Like German beers, the local version ranges from medium to fairly heavy. For a non-alcoholic drink, try one of the excellent local fruit juices, particularly apple and grape juice. Mineral water, still or bubbly, Swiss or imported, is found everywhere.

After dinner, Swiss fruit brandies are popular. Distilled from apples, plums, cherries or pears, these colourless potions pack a punch.

Coffee

The Swiss drink small cups of coffee, often adding cream, but for breakfast it's usually *Milchkaffee,* coffee with hot milk (called *renversée* in the French-speaking section). Swiss coffee is generally weaker than French or Italian brews but stronger than American coffee. In Switzerland espresso goes by the Italian name, *ristretto*.

BERLITZ-INFO

CONTENTS

A ACCOMMODATION

Hotels of all categories are listed in the *Swiss Hotel Guide* issued annually by the Swiss Hotel Association. You can find the publication at Swiss National Tourist Offices abroad as well as at many travel agencies. The tourist office also distributes the *Swiss Hotel Guide for the Disabled* and a brochure entitled *Historical Inns and Castle Hotels.* In Switzerland local tourist offices will supply you with last-minute details and offer suggestions for all types of accommodation from luxury hotels to modest, family-run establishments. If you want to steer a middle course on accommodation, book a room at a *hôtel garni,* which provides bed but not board, permitting you to eat out more adventurously.

Hotels of all classifications in Switzerland are usually very clean and provide all the essentials. Rates include taxes, service charges and continental breakfast. You must show your passport and fill in a form when registering. Remember that prices are usually quoted per person and not by the room.

Private rooms. Local tourist offices maintain lists of rooms to let in private homes—the Swiss equivalent of bed-and-breakfast establishments. Or take your chances and stop at a house with a *"Zimmer"* or *"Chambres à louer"* sign outside. (Most such accommodation is in German-speaking Switzerland.)

Chalets and flats. For family holidays, particularly in mountain resorts, self-catering flats and chalets may be rented through agencies abroad or on the spot.

Youth hostels. There is no maximum age, though members 25 and under have priority. Advance booking is recommended in summer and in popular winter sports regions. In the cities certain hostels are closed in winter. For addresses and regulations, write to Schweizerischer Bund für Jugendherbergen

Hochhaus 9, Shopping-Center, Postfach 132, 8958 Spreitenbach

Camping. Several hundred campsites, some high in the Alps, are approved by the Swiss Camping and Caravan Association. For a list

154

of sites, facilities and rates, write to Schweizerischer Camping- und Caravanning-Verband (SCCV)

Habsburgerstrasse 35, 6000 Lucerne 4.

(*Note:* Camping on private property or outside a recognized campsite requires special permission.)

I'd like...	Ich möchte...	J'aimerais...	Vorrei...
a single/double room	ein Einzel-/ Doppel- zimmer	une chambre à un lit/ à deux lits	una camera singola/ doppia
with bath/ shower	mit Bad/ Dusche	avec bains/ douche	con bagno/ doccia
What's the rate per night?	Was kostet eine Über- nachtung?	Quel est le prix pour une nuit?	Quanto costa per notte?

AIRPORTS

Switzerland's three major international airports are, in order of importance, Zurich-Kloten, Geneva-Cointrin and Basle/Mulhouse. The Swiss national airline provides frequent flights between these airports, and there are convenient rail connections as well. Small airports serve Berne and Lugano.

Generally, passengers must check in 45 minutes before flight time—consult your airline to be sure. The three major airports have snack bars and restaurants, news-stands, car-hire desks, banks, post offices, duty-free shops and boutiques. Self-service luggage carts may be found in the baggage-claim area.

Ground transport. A frequent train service links Zurich-Kloten—there's a station in the terminal building itself—to the city's main railway station, a 10-minute trip. Direct trains to and from the airport also serve many other Swiss cities.

Airport coaches operate from the other airports to the city centres—every 20 minutes in Geneva and half an hour in Basle and Berne. Every hour and a half there is an airport coach from Geneva-Cointrin to Lausanne, the trip takes 50 minutes.

Fly Luggage. If you're departing from Zurich or Geneva on a scheduled or charter flight, you can register baggage all the way to your final destination at many Swiss railway and postal bus stations. The service is called Fly Luggage (*Fly-Gepäck/Bagages-Fly/Bagaglio Fly*). A small charge is made per piece—well worth it, considering the aggravation saved. You may be required to check your baggage in up to 24 hours in advance. You must show your air ticket.

Where's the bus for...?	Wo fährt der Bus nach... ab?	D'où part le bus pour...?	Da dove parte l'autobus per...?

B BABY-SITTERS

Your hotel receptionist can usually arrange for a reliable baby-sitter. Many resorts have nurseries geared to take care of small children while you ski. In the big towns, department stores often provide staffed nurseries for shoppers.

Can you get me a baby-sitter for tonight?	Können Sie mir für heute abend einen Babysitter besorgen?	Pouvez-vous me trouver un(e) babysitter pour ce soir?	Può trovarmi una bambinaia per questa sera?

C CIGARETTES, CIGARS, TOBACCO

Some well-known European and American brands of cigarettes are manufactured under licence in Switzerland, in addition to scores of local makes. On sale at tobacconists, news-stands, etc., cigarettes are relatively cheap in Switzerland.

Pipe and cigar smokers will find every kind of tobacco and cigars from the world over, including the best Cuban brands.

Smoking is banned in cinemas and on most public transport. On trains, smoking is limited to designated sections.

CLIMATE AND CLOTHING

Temperatures can vary within a few miles, a few hundred feet of altitude, or a few hours of the day—so it's best to be prepared for every eventuality. In summer bring a raincoat or umbrella and a warm jacket or sweater—just in case. In winter you'll be grateful for a weatherproof coat, and—if you're in the mountains—snow boots. For ski areas sunglasses are important to protect your eyes from the glare.

The Swiss dress conservatively in subdued colours and modest styles. In a smart restaurant you may feel out of step without jacket and tie, but generally speaking casual clothing is appropriate.

Average daily minimum and maximum temperatures in degrees Celsius:

		J	F	M	A	M	J	J	A	S	O	N	D
Zurich	min.	–3	–2	1	4	8	12	14	13	10	6	2	–2
	max.	2	5	10	15	20	23	25	24	21	14	7	3
Geneva	min.	–2	–1	2	5	9	13	14	14	11	7	3	0
	max.	4	6	10	15	19	23	25	25	21	14	8	4
Lugano	min.	–2	–1	2	6	10	14	16	15	13	8	3	0
	max.	6	9	13	17	21	25	28	27	23	16	10	7

And in degrees Fahrenheit:

		J	F	M	A	M	J	J	A	S	O	N	D
Zurich	min.	27	28	34	39	46	54	57	55	50	43	36	28
	max.	36	41	50	59	68	73	77	75	70	57	45	37
Geneva	min.	28	30	36	41	48	55	57	57	52	45	37	32
	max.	39	43	50	59	66	73	77	77	70	57	46	39
Lugano	min.	28	30	36	43	50	57	61	59	55	46	37	32
	max.	43	48	55	63	70	77	82	81	73	61	50	45

COMMUNICATIONS

Post offices display a distinctive sign bearing the letters, PTT *(Post, Telegraf, Telefon)*. In addition to normal postal business, they handle telephone calls, telegrams and most of Switzerland's money transfers. Most post offices are open from around 7.30 a.m. to 6 (small branches) or 6.30 p.m. with a break for lunch, and on Saturday mornings from 7.30 to 11 a.m. In bigger towns the main post office does not close at midday, and a window may be open until 10 p.m. or even later, and at weekends, for express or special delivery mail.

If you don't know in advance where you'll be staying in Switzerland, you can have mail sent to the poste restante or general delivery desk *(Postlagernd/poste restante/fermo posta)* at the main post office of any town you expect to visit. You'll have to show your passport when collecting mail.

After hours you can buy stamps from vending machines outside post offices and some train stations, as well as in souvenir shops and at hotel reception desks. Letter boxes are yellow.

Telegrams and telex. Main post offices accept telegrams and telex messages from 7.30 a.m. to 10 p.m. To send a telegram by telephone, call from your hotel—dial 110 (round the clock). The charge will be added to your bill.

Telephone. The Swiss telephone network is automated and efficient, and street-corner coin telephones are kept clean and in good working order. Coin phones carry instructions in four languages (including English). You can dial international (but not overseas) calls from a coin phone. To make overseas calls from a public phone, you have to go to the post office. Ask for a phone, wait for the dial tone and dial the number directly; you pay at the window afterwards. Coin phones are also found in all post offices.

express (special delivery)	*Express*	*par exprès*	*espresso*
airmail	*Luftpost*	*par avion*	*via aerea*
registered	*Einschreiben*	*recommandé*	*raccomandata*
a stamp	*eine Brief-marke*	*un timbre*	*un franco-bollo*
I want to send a tele-gram to...	*Ich möchte ein Telegramm nach... aufgeben.*	*J'aimerais envoyer un télégramme à...*	*Vorrei mandare un telegramma a...*

COMPLAINTS
Switzerland's tourist industry prides itself on competent and courteous service. Complaints are taken seriously. A word to the hotel or restaurant manager should sort out any problems there; if not, contact the local tourist office.

CRIME AND THEFT
Muggings and crimes of violence are rare in Switzerland, where you can come and go, day and night, in peace. But burglars, pickpockets and associated operatives can strike in any country, so it's always wise to lock your car and put your valuables in the hotel safe. Sneak thieves have even begun stealing skis from atop cars and from the entrances of après-ski spots.

CUSTOMS AND ENTRY REGULATIONS
Most visitors—including citizens of Britain, the United States and the majority of other English-speaking countries—need only a valid passport to enter Switzerland. British subjects can use the simplified Visitor's Passport. Without further formality you are generally entitled to stay for up to 90 days.

There is no restriction on the import or export of either Swiss or foreign currencies.

The following chart shows what main duty-free items you may take into Switzerland and, when returning home, into your own country.

Into:	Cigarettes	Cigars	Tobacco	Spirits	Wine
Switzer-land*	200 (400)	or 50 (100)	or 250 g. (500 g.)	1 l. and	2 l.
Australia	200	or 250 g.	or 250 g.	1 l. or	1 l.
Canada	200	and 50	and 900 g.	1.1 l. or	1.1 l.
Eire	200	or 50	or 250 g.	1 l. and	2 l.
N. Zealand	200	or 50	or ½ lb.	1 qt. and	1 qt.
S. Africa	400	and 50	and 250 g.	1 l. and	1 l.
U.K.	200	or 50	or 250 g.	1 l. and	2 l.
U.S.A.	200	and 100	and **	1 l. or	1 l.

* The figures in parentheses are for non-European visitors only.
** A reasonable quantity.

I have nothing to declare.	*Ich habe nichts zu verzollen.*	*Je n'ai rien à déclarer.*	*Non ho nulla da dichiarare.*
It's for my personal use.	*Das ist für meinen persönlichen Gebrauch.*	*C'est pour mon usage personnel.*	*È per mio uso personale.*

ELECTRIC CURRENT
E

Standard voltage throughout Switzerland is 220-volt 50-cycle A.C. Check your appliances to see whether a plug adaptor or transformer will be required.

EMBASSIES AND CONSULATES
All embassies in the Swiss capital, Berne, have consular sections (for passport renewal, visas, etc.). Some countries maintain consulates in Geneva, Zurich and other towns.

Australia. Alpenstrasse 29, 3006 Berne; tel. (031) 43 01 43
Consulate: Rue de Moillebeau 56-58, 1209 Geneva; tel. (022) 34 62 00

Canada. Kirchenfeldstrasse 88, 3005 Berne; tel. (031) 44 63 81
Consulate: Avenue de Budé 8, 1201 Geneva; tel. (022) 33 90 00

Eire. Eigerstrasse 71, 3007 Berne; tel. (031) 46 23 53

South Africa. Jungfraustrasse 1, 3005 Berne, tel. (031) 44 20 11
Consulate: Bleicherweg 58, 8002 Zurich; tel. (01) 201 45 40

United Kingdom. Thunstrasse 50, 3005 Berne; tel. (031) 44 50 21
Consulates: Rue de Vermont 37-39, 1202 Geneva; tel. (022) 34 38 00
Bellerivestrasse 5, 8008 Zurich; tel. (01) 47 15 20

U.S.A. Jubiläumsstrasse 93, 3005 Berne; tel. (031) 43 70 11
Consulates: Route de Pregny 11, 1292 Chambésy/Geneva;
tel. (022) 99 02 11.
Zollikerstrasse 141, 8008 Zurich; tel. (01) 55 25 66

EMERGENCIES
Police   117   Fire   118

For other emergency numbers dial the information service—111—or
look in the blue pages in the front of any telephone directory.

For the name and address of a pharmacy on 24-hour duty, consult
the day's local paper; the address is also posted in the window of all
chemist's shops *(Apotheke/pharmacie/farmacia)*.

G GETTING AROUND SWITZERLAND

By Car
Rental. To hire a car you must produce a valid driving licence, held
for a minimum of one year. You must be at least 21 years old
(sometimes 25). You can hire a car at many railway stations. Agencies usually waive cash deposits for clients with authorized credit
cards. If you want to return the car outside Switzerland, you'll be
charged extra.

Driving your own car. To bring your car into Switzerland, you'll
need a national driving licence, car registration papers and Green
Card (a recommended but not obligatory extension to your regular
insurance policy, validating it for foreign countries).

A nationality code sticker must be visible at the rear of your car,
and you must have a red reflector warning triangle for use in case of a
breakdown. If you wear glasses you are required to carry an extra
pair. Seat belts are obligatory.

In winter you may be required to use snow chains on Alpine
passes. These can be obtained at filling stations along the way.

On the road. Drive on the right and give priority to the right unless
otherwise indicated. On mountain roads leave the awesome views to
the passengers; to admire the scenery in safety, stop at roadside

parking areas. On difficult stretches of mountain roads, priority is given to postal buses—otherwise to the ascending vehicle. Sounding your horn is recommended on blind corners of mountain roads; avoid it everywhere else.

In general roads are good. A well-developed motorway (expressway) network links all the big towns. Motorists who use the motorways must purchase a sticker (valid for one year) to be displayed on the windscreen. Failure to comply will result in a heavy fine.

Speed limits. On the green signposted motorways *(Autobahn/autoroute/autostrada)*, the maximum speed is 120 kph (kilometres per hour)—about 75 mph. On other roads the limit is 80 kph (about 50 mph) unless otherwise indicated. In residential areas the speed limit is restricted to 50 kph (about 30 mph). Cars towing caravans (trailers) may not exceed 80 kph (50 mph), even on motorways.

Breakdowns. If you have a breakdown, call TCS *(Touring-Club der Schweiz/Touring Club Suisse/Touring Club Svizzero)*. Members of any affiliated automobile association will not be charged for service. Otherwise you'll have to pay the full bill for the help of a serviceman or patrolman. On the motorways there are emergency telephones at regular intervals. Or go to the nearest public telephone and dial 140 for help.

Parking. Try to avoid congested central shopping and medieval "old town" districts. Most cities have parking meters and blue zones—the outlines of parking spaces are painted blue—where parking is limited to 1½ hours. In zones marked in red you can park for up to 15 hours. To park in either zone you must display a disc *(Parkscheibe/disque de stationnement/disco orario)* on the dashboard indicating when you left your car. Discs are available free at filling stations and banks.

Road signs. Most signs in Switzerland are familiar international pictographs. Following are a few others you might come across:

Auffahrt	Entrée	Entrata	**Entrance**
Ausfahrt	Sortie	Uscita	**Exit**
Flughafen	Aéroport	Aeroporto	**Airport**
Glatteisgefahr	Verglas	Strada ghiacciata	**Icy road**
Stadtzentrum	Centre-ville	Centro città	**City centre**
Umleitung	Déviation	Deviazione	**Diversion (detour)**
Zoll	Douane	Dogana	**Customs**

driving licence	Führerausweis	permis de conduire	licenza di condurre
car registration papers	Fahrzeug-ausweis	permis de circulation	licenza di circolazione
Fill the tank, please.	Volltanken, bitte.	Le plein, s'il vous plaît.	Il pieno, per favore.
I've had a breakdown.	Ich habe eine Panne.	Ma voiture est en panne.	La mia auto ha un guasto.
There's been an accident.	Es ist ein Un-fall passiert.	Il y a eu un accident.	C'è stato un incidente.

By Train

Swiss trains are fast, clean, comfortable and very punctual. If there are any delays, they usually follow heavy snowfalls. Trains run at fixed intervals, with regular hourly service between all major centres. Apart from the Swiss Holiday Card (see pp. 163-4) reductions are available in the form of excursion tickets and circular tickets. The Skipass is good for rail travel to certain resorts plus unlimited use of ski lifts.

Visitors from outside Europe may travel on the Eurailpass, a flat-rate unlimited mileage ticket, valid for first-class rail travel anywhere in Western Europe outside Great Britain. Eurail Youthpass offers second-class travel at a cheaper rate to travellers under 26.

Travellers aged 16 to 26 and women over 62 and men over 65 can apply for an Inter-Rail Card, valid for one month of second-class train travel in some 20 European countries.

Some Swiss rail terminology:

Intercity: Air-conditioned express, major cities only.

Schnellzug (Train direct, treno diretto): Express, stops at big and medium-sized towns.

Regionalzug (Train régional, treno regionale): Local, stops at all stations.

By Postal Bus

Wherever the trains don't go, the bright yellow postal buses do. They carry mail and passengers—the local population and sightseers—over mountain roads to the smallest of hamlets. The drivers inspire confidence on any road in any weather: after all, in the entire history of the system, there's only been one accident—a bump. Advance seat reservations are made free of charge.

By Boat

Sizable passenger boats, often with restaurants, ply all the big lakes; one line on the Lake of Geneva *(Lac Léman)* provides the fastest means of transport to France, across the way. In some cases you can make the return trip by train. Local tourist offices have maps, timetables and advice. Remember that the Eurailpass is valid for travel by boat.

Local Transport

Swiss cities have efficient public transport networks (buses, trolley-buses, trams). Before boarding the bus, buy a ticket from a vending machine—there's one at nearly every stop—otherwise enter at the front and buy one from the driver. Hold on to it in case an inspector makes a spot check at some point during your trip. On many vehicles you must press a button to open the door to get on or off.

Tourists intending to make intensive use of buses or trams can save money by purchasing a one-day ticket *(Tageskarte/abonnement d'un jour/abbonamento giornaliero)* for 24 hours of unlimited travel on a town's public transport network. These tickets are sold at principal bus stops or the main railway station. A variation is the one-day Multi-City Card, valid on the same day in several different towns.

Taxi

You might try hailing a taxi on the street, but a better bet may be going to a taxi rank at a major hotel or the railway station; or you can telephone for a cab. The fares, which vary from town to town, are never low. Cabs are metered and there are set prices for extras such as baggage. A service charge is included in the fare in many towns, such as Geneva, Zurich, Berne and Basle; elsewhere 15% is customary.

Bicycle

You can hire a bicycle at the railway station in any sizable town in Switzerland and return it to any other station at no extra charge. At smaller stations it's advisable to book a bike a day in advance. Tourist offices distribute leaflets describing special cycle routes.

Swiss Holiday Card

You can criss-cross the whole country with a Swiss Holiday Card *(Schweizer Ferienkarte/Carte Suisse de Vacances/Tessera Svizzera di Vacanze)*, valid for 4, 8, 15 days or 1 month of unlimited travel on the federal railway network, plus scores of private railways, nine boat lines and 120 postal bus routes. Good for discounts on mountain railways, aerial cableways, etc., the card offers convenience and significant savings for travellers resident outside Switzerland. Apply for the card at travel agencies or Swiss tourist offices abroad, and at major railway stations in Switzerland. You must show your passport.

first/second class	erste/zweite Klasse	première/ deuxième classe	prima/seconda classe
single (one way)/return (round-trip)	einfach/retour	simple course/ aller-retour	andata/andata e ritorno
Where's the nearest bus stop?	Wo ist die nächste Bus-haltestelle?	Où se trouve l'arrêt de bus le plus proche?	Dove si trova la fermata d'autobus più vicina?

GETTING TO SWITZERLAND

Due to the complexity and variability of the many fares, you should consult an informed travel agent well before your trip.

From North America

Daily non-stop flights link New York to Zurich and Geneva, the main gateway cities; connecting service operates to Basle. Daily non-stop flights are available from Montreal to Zurich; a dozen Canadian cities offer connecting service. There are frequent domestic flights and good train service between the three major airports of Switzerland.

You can travel first class, business or economy class, or on a variety of special fares, including APEX (Advance Purchase Excursion) and Excursion. Children up to the age of 12 fly for a significant discount.

Charters and package tours. Advance Booking Charters (ABC) must be booked 60 days before departure. The One-Stop Inclusive Tour Charter (OTC) combines transport accommodation and excursions. Complete package tours (including flights) to cities or ski resorts for 7 to 14 days or longer include choice of hotels and options for renting a car or purchasing a Eurailpass.

From Great Britain and Eire

By air. Regular scheduled flights leave daily from London for Zurich, Geneva and Basle, with additional service from London to Berne. Non-stop flights operate from Manchester to Zurich (daily) and from Birmingham to Zurich and Geneva (several times a week).

There are also non-stop connections from Dublin to Zurich and Geneva; weekly service links Cork and Zurich.

Special fares include excursion tickets valid for one month (must stay away on a Saturday night) and budget (one-way or return), PEX and APEX fares. Certain airlines offer fly/drive or fly/rail combinations.

Package tours. There are frequent departures for Zurich, Basle and Geneva, as well as a wide range of accommodation—from youth hostel or bed-and-breakfast to full board in a five-star hotel, with skiing or hiking arrangements included. Cancellation conditions are often stringent, so take out insurance.

By rail. The journey from London normally takes about 18 hours. Change in Paris for the French "bullet train", the *TGV*, to Geneva or Lausanne; it cruises at 260 kilometres per hour (160 mph). Couchettes or sleepers should be reserved in advance. The Swiss National Tourist Office has information on reduced-fare train travel.

By road. Book passage on car ferries well in advance. Fares are cheaper for midweek sailings; the price fluctuates seasonally. The best route is Calais–Rimes–Chaumont–Basle–Zurich, or Calais/Boulogne–Paris–Geneva. Regular coach service between London (Victoria) and Geneva operates several times a week; the trip takes roughly 20 hours.

From the Southern Hemisphere

Australia. Scheduled flights serve the main cities, but you must change planes either in the Far East or in Europe. Special fares include excursion (minimum stay 21 days), one-way excursion and student deals.

New Zealand. Flights operate daily to Switzerland with one change en route. Excursion fares allow for a stopover.

South Africa. You can travel direct to Switzerland several times a week. Save on regular fares by booking an excursion (with or without stopovers) or PEX (fixed date) ticket. Many package tours to Europe include Switzerland on the itinerary.

HAIRDRESSERS AND BARBERS   H
In major towns and resorts, first-class hair stylists can always be found. Prices tend to be high, but there's no need to tip: a 15% service charge is included in the bill. Note that many establishments close Mondays, some mornings only, others all day.

haircut	Haarschnitt	coupe	taglio
shampoo and set/blow-dry	Waschen und Legen/Föhnen	shampooing et mise en plis/ brushing	lavaggio dei capelli e messa in piega/asciuga-tura al fono
permanent wave	Dauerwelle	permanente	permanente
colour rinse	Tönen	un rinçage	un riflesso
dye	Färben	une teinture	una tintura

HEALTH AND MEDICAL CARE

Most major resorts have clinics, and all cities are served by modern, well-equipped hospitals. The standard of treatment is high, especially when it comes to ski-related injuries. Since health care can be very expensive, seek advice from your travel agency or insurance company about a policy covering illness or accident on holiday; or your travel agent can put you in touch with one of the Swiss insurance firms.

Any pharmacist can recommend and supply remedies for minor ailments and advise you where to find a doctor if you need one (see also EMERGENCIES).

Yes, you can drink the water!

I need a doctor/ dentist.	Ich brauche einen Arzt/ Zahnarzt.	Il me faut un médecin/un dentiste.	Ho bisogno di un medico/un dentista.
I have a pain here.	Es tut mir hier weh.	J'ai mal ici.	Mi fa male qui.
I have a sore throat/fever.	Ich habe Hals-weh/Fieber.	J'ai mal à la gorge/J'ai de la fièvre.	Mi fa male la gola/Ho la feb-bre.

HITCH-HIKING

Autostop, as it is called in German, French and Italian, is legal everywhere in Switzerland except on the motorways (expressways). On the whole, the country's a fairly good hunting ground for anyone looking for a lift.

Can you give me a lift to...?	Können Sie mich bis... mitnehmen?	Pouvez-vous m'emmener à...?	Può darmi un passaggio fino a...?

HOURS

Most offices open from 8 a.m. or even earlier until noon and from 1.30 to 5 p.m. or later, Monday to Friday. Shops and stores open from 8 a.m. to 6.30 or 7 p.m.; the smaller establishments close for lunch. Shops large and small have a half-day closing, perhaps Monday morning, or Wednesday or Thursday afternoon. On Saturdays many open non-stop from around 8 a.m. until 5 or 5.30 p.m. During the tourist season, summer and winter, some shops in alpine resorts open Sundays as well.

Museum hours can vary considerably, but in general they are 10 a.m. to noon and 2 to 5 or 6 p.m. See also COMMUNICATIONS and MONEY MATTERS.

LANGUAGE   L

Switzerland has four official languages—German, French, Italian and the rare Romansh. So it's only natural that the Swiss tend to be talented at learning foreign languages, and a great many people speak English well enough to help you find your way around.

Many towns, lakes, villages, etc., bear different names in German and French (not to mention Italian and Romansh). Signposts and maps can baffle the stranger. Here are a few variations to bear in mind:

English	German	French
Basle	*Basel*	*Bâle*
Bienne	*Biel*	*Bienne*
Lake Constance	*Bodensee*	*Lac de Constance*
Chur	*Chur*	*Coire*
Fribourg	*Freiburg*	*Fribourg*
Geneva	*Genf*	*Genève*
Lake Geneva	*Genfersee*	*Lac Léman*
Grisons	*Graubünden*	*Grisons*
Lucerne	*Luzern*	*Lucerne*
Lake Lucerne	*Vierwald-stättersee*	*Lac des Quatre-Cantons*
Matterhorn	*Matterhorn*	*Cervin*
Neuchâtel	*Neuenburg*	*Neuchâtel*
Solothurn	*Solothurn*	*Soleure*

The Berlitz phrase books GERMAN FOR TRAVELLERS, FRENCH FOR TRAVELLERS and ITALIAN FOR TRAVELLERS cover almost all situations you're likely to encounter in Switzerland. In addition, the Berlitz pocket dictionaries of German, French and Italian each contain a glossary of 12,500 terms plus a menu reader supplement.

| Do you speak English? | Sprechen Sie Englisch? | Parlez-vous anglais? | Parla inglese? |

LAUNDRY AND DRY-CLEANING
Most hotels provide reliable laundry *(Wäscherei/blanchisserie/ lavanderia)* and dry-cleaning *(Chemische Reinigung/nettoyage à sec/lavaggio a secco)* services. Sizable towns and holiday resorts have facilities, but you cannot count on dry-cleaning services in the smaller resorts. Self-service launderettes are the exception, not the rule.

LOST PROPERTY
Check first with your hotel receptionist, then report the loss to the nearest police station. In honest Switzerland there's a very good chance of recovering lost property. Reclaim articles left behind on trains or buses at the railway or public transport lost property office *(Fundbüro/bureau des objets trouvés/ufficio oggetti smarriti)*. Customarily a reward equivalent to 10% of the value must be paid to the finder.

| I've lost my wallet/handbag/ passport. | Ich habe mein Portemonnaie/ meine Hand- tasche/meinen Pass verloren. | J'ai perdu mon porte-monnaie/ mon sac à main/ mon passeport. | Ho perso il portafoglio/ la borsetta/ il passaporto. |

M MAPS
A selection of regional maps and road maps are on sale at stationers and bookshops. Tourist offices, car-hire agencies and the larger banks distribute excellent town plans. Hikers should ask for the indispensable maps of the Federal Topographical Survey.

The maps in this guide were prepared by Hallwag AG, Berne. Hallwag also produces a variety of large-scale maps of Switzerland.

| a town plan | ein Stadtplan | un plan de ville | una pianta della città |
| a (road) map | eine (Strassen) Karte | une carte (routière) | una carta (stradale) |

MEETING PEOPLE

The Swiss, though friendly, tend to be reserved, so it may take some persistence to make contact. But the scene is more relaxed in the resorts.

In social as well as business situations, punctuality is considered most important. If you should be invited to a Swiss home for dinner, don't forget flowers or sweets for the hostess.

Entering and leaving small shops or offices, be sure to say hello, goodbye, please and thank you; the Swiss are very polite. An important Swiss-German expression is *Grüezi (mitenand),* meaning roughly "Hello (everybody)!". The equivalent departure phrase would be the hybrid *Adieu mitenand* ("So long, everybody!"). You may also hear the Swiss-German for "goodbye", *Uf Wiederluege.* Otherwise, schoolbook German, French and Italian suffice. See also LANGUAGE and USEFUL EXPRESSIONS.

MONEY MATTERS

Currency. The monetary unit of Switzerland is the Swiss franc (abbreviated Fr.), divided into 100 centimes (abbreviated *Rp.*—for *Rappen*—in German and *c.* in French and Italian). Coins are minted in 5-, 10-, 20- and 50-centime pieces as well as 1-, 2- and 5-franc pieces. Banknotes come in denominations of 10, 20, 50, 100, 500 and 1,000 francs.

Banks. Most banks are open weekdays from 8.30 a. m. to 12.30 p.m. and again from 1.30 to 4.30 or 5.30 p.m. Main branches generally remain open during the lunch hour. One day a week, branches keep slightly later hours, till 6 or 6.30 p.m., the day varying from town to town. In Zurich the big banking day is Monday. Currency exchange offices at airports and the larger railway stations do business from around 6.30 a.m. to 9 p.m. (sometimes even later) every day of the week.

Credit cards. Smaller businesses don't like to deal with credit cards, but they're widely accepted in major establishments; you'll find the signs prominently displayed at the entrance.

Traveller's cheques. Banks will give you a better rate of exchange than shops, hotels and restaurants, but the well-known international cheques are generally accepted everywhere. You must show your passport when cashing one.

I want to change some pounds/dollars.	Ich möchte einige Pfund/ Dollars wechseln.	Je voudrais changer des livres sterling/ dollars.	Vorrei cambiare delle sterline/ dei dollari.
Do you accept traveller's cheques?	Nehmen Sie Reiseschecks?	Acceptez-vous les chèques de voyage?	Accetta assegni turistici?
Can I pay with this credit card?	Kann ich mit dieser Kredit- karte bezahlen?	Puis-je payer avec cette carte de crédit?	Posso pagare con questa carta di credito?

N NEWSPAPERS AND MAGAZINES

Even in small towns, news-stands stock a surprisingly ample variety of foreign papers, plus all the Swiss newspapers. The best selection and earliest delivery are offered by main railway stations and airports. The British dailies and the *International Herald Tribune* (edited in Paris, printed in Zurich) are widely available, along with magazines of all kinds.

Have you any English- language newspapers?	Haben Sie englisch- sprachige Zeitungen?	Avez-vous des journaux en anglais?	Ha giornali in inglese?

P PHOTOGRAPHY

Swiss dealers handle all the popular brands and sizes of film. Photo shops in the large mountain resorts develop and print black-and-white film, but colour film usually has to be mailed to city labs. Major stores also accept film for processing.

I'd like film for this camera.	Ich möchte einen Film für diesen Apparat.	J'aimerais un film pour cet appareil.	Vorrei una pelli- cola per questa macchina foto- grafica.
black-and-white film	einen Schwarz- weissfilm	un film noir et blanc	una pellicola in bianco e nero
film for colour prints	einen Farb- film	un film couleurs	una pellicola a colori
colour-slide film	einen Diafilm	un film pour diapositives	una pellicola per diapositive

POLICE

Switzerland has no uniformed federal police. Law and order is the responsibility of the individual cantons and communities, and thus the uniforms vary greatly from place to place. Police are armed, efficient and courteous; law enforcement is strict.

The emergency telephone number for the police is 117.

Where's the nearest police station?	*Wo ist der nächste Polizeiposten?*	*Où est le poste de police le plus proche?*	*Dove si trova il posto di polizia più vicino?*

PRICES

Some prices may be slightly higher in the elite resorts and in Zurich and Geneva, but otherwise they vary only slightly from one region to another.

To give you an idea of what to expect, here are some average prices in Swiss francs. Despite the country's low inflation rate, all prices must be regarded as approximate.

Bicycle hire. 4 hours Fr. 6, 12 hours Fr. 9, 24 hours Fr. 12.

Buses. Fr. 0.70 for up to 3 stops, Fr. 1.20 for 4 stops or more. 1-day ticket Fr. 3.50, 3-day tourist pass Fr. 8.

Car hire. *Renault 5TL* Fr. 35 per day, Fr. 0.47 per kilometre, Fr. 490 per week with unlimited mileage. *Ford Escort* Fr. 58 per day, Fr. 0.65 per km., Fr. 750 per week with unlimited mileage.

Cigarettes. Fr. 1.90–2.90 for a packet of 20.

Hairdressers. *Man's* haircut Fr. 20–30. *Woman's* cut Fr. 23–30, shampoo and set Fr. 20–25, shampoo and blow-dry Fr. 25–30, permanent wave Fr. 60–70.

Meals and drinks. Continental breakfast Fr. 6–8, lunch/dinner in fairly good establishment Fr. 15–30, cheese *fondue* from Fr. 12, coffee Fr. 1.70, glass of beer Fr. 1.70, ½ litre of table wine Fr. 8–12, soft drinks Fr. 2.50.

Ski-equipment hire. Cross-country from Fr. 15 a day, Fr. 70 a week. Downhill from Fr. 30 a day, Fr. 125–150 a week.

Swiss Holiday Card (2nd class). Fr. 125 for 4 days, Fr. 150 for 8 days, Fr. 190 for 15 days, Fr. 265 for a month.

Taxis. Meter charge Fr. 4, plus Fr. 1.30 minimum per kilometre.

Trains (2nd class, single/one way). Zurich–Geneva Fr. 46, Geneva–Lausanne Fr. 12.80.

PUBLIC HOLIDAYS

In decentralized Switzerland the calendar of holidays varies from canton to canton. On the following days, banks and shops are closed everywhere:

January 1	*Neujahr/Nouvel An/Capodanno*	New Year's Day
December 25	*Weihnachten/Noël/Natale*	Christmas Day
Movable Dates:	*Karfreitag/Vendredi-Saint/ Venerdì Santo*	Good Friday
	Auffahrt/Ascension/Ascensione	Ascension

In addition, Easter Monday and Whit Monday are celebrated in many cantons. On August 1, the national day of Switzerland, businesses close for at least half, if not all, the day.

Are you open tomorrow?	*Haben Sie morgen offen?*	*Ouvrez-vous demain?*	*È aperto domani?*

R RADIO AND TV

Many hotel rooms have radios that relay BBC news in English at certain hours, as well as the English programmes of Swiss Radio International, the shortwave service based in Berne. You can also tune in to the Swiss channels broadcasting in German, French and Italian.

On transistor sets you may be able to pick up the BBC and other European stations, as well as the American Forces Network.

Swiss TV has German-, French- and Italian-language channels; depending on where you are, you may also be able to pick up the networks of West Germany, Austria, France and Italy.

RELIGIOUS SERVICES

Switzerland is almost equally divided between Roman Catholics and Protestants, but many other faiths are represented in the major cities. Times of service or mass are posted on roadside signboards on the outskirts. In bigger towns it's best to consult the local newspaper or ask your hotel receptionist.

English and American congregations are to be found in bigger towns and resorts.

RESTAURANTS

In Switzerland you'll find restaurants of every kind, from simple country taverns to elegant five-star establishments. In winter you can thaw out in a rustic, wood-panelled *carnotzet* or a cosy country inn *(Gasthof)*. In spring, lakeside restaurants open their terraces. Mountainside restaurants combine *haute cuisine* with high altitude and dazzling views. The *grotti* of Ticino are little home-style eating houses tucked away in unexpected spots. Geneva's *brasseries* are bright and cheery. In Zurich the guildhalls offer history and gastronomy. And Berne's cellars *(Keller)* are rich in medieval atmosphere.

In all regions there is a proliferation of Italian-style restaurants featuring pizza and pasta, as well as American-type fast-food emporia. Cuisines as exotic as Chinese, Greek, Indian, North African and Vietnamese are available in the more cosmopolitan towns. The dish of the day *(Tagessteller, assiette du jour, piatto del giorno)* is usually served quickly, and you'll pay less.

As a general rule, lunch is available from noon to 1.30 p.m. and dinner from 7 to 9.30 p.m. Hot food can rarely be obtained outside these hours, but snacks and cold dishes usually can.

Prices tend to be high but honest and—given the standards of living and the cost of raw materials—not unreasonable. Many restaurants operate a café section where good food is served at moderate prices. A Swiss peculiarity: in most popular restaurants and cafés, as you eat and drink, cash-register tickets are placed on your table. At the end of the meal the waiter or waitress will add them up, tell you how much you owe and collect the money. (If the server is going off duty early, don't be surprised if the bill is presented while you are still eating.)

A service charge is included in the price in all cafés and restaurants. But for very good service you may leave a few coins in addition.

Asking the waiter (in German, French and Italian)

Could we have a table?	Wir hätten gern einen Tisch.	Pouvons-nous avoir une table?	Possiamo avere un tavolo?
Do you have a set menu?	Haben Sie ein Tagesmenü?	Avez-vous un menu du jour?	Ha il menù del giorno?
I'd like...	Ich möchte...	J'aimerais...	Vorrei...
beer	ein Bier	une bière	una birra
bread	etwas Brot	du pain	del pane
coffee	einen Kaffee	un café	un caffè
fish	Fisch	du poisson	del pesce

173

Asking the waiter...

meat	Fleisch	de la viande	della carne
potatoes	Kartoffeln	des pommes de terre	delle patate
sugar	Zucker	du sucre	dello zucchero
tea	einen Tee	un thé	un té
wine	Wein	du vin	del vino

Reading the menu in German...

Bohnen	beans	Lamm	lamb
Bratwurst	grilled veal sausage	Leber	liver
		Poulet	chicken
Crevetten	prawns	Ragout	stew
Ei(er)	egg(s)	Rahm	cream
Erbsen	peas	Rindfleisch	beef
Erdbeeren	strawberries	Schinken	ham
Forelle	trout	Schlagrahm	whipped cream
gebacken	baked	Schweinefleisch	pork
gebraten	roasted	Spargeln	asparagus
gekocht	boiled	Teigwaren	noodles
Kalbfleisch	veal	Torte	layer cake
Käse	cheese	Wienerli	frankfurter
Kuchen	cake	Zitrone	lemon
Lachs	salmon	Zwiebeln	onions

and French...

agneau	lamb	lard	bacon
asperges	asparagus	macédoine de fruits	fruit salad
bœuf	beef	médaillon	tenderloin
canard	duck	œufs	eggs
champignons	mushrooms	pomme	apple
chasse	game	porc	pork
chevreuil	venison	poulet	chicken
côte(lette)	chop, cutlet	raisins	grapes
entrecôte	steak	saucisse/ saucisson	sausage
foie	liver		
fraises	strawberries	saumon (fumé)	(smoked) salmon
gigot (d'agneau)	leg of lamb		
glace	ice-cream	terrine	paté
haricots verts	green beans	truite	trout
jambon	ham	veau	veal

174

and Italian...

agnello	*lamb*	**gelato**	*ice-cream*
asparagi	*asparagus*	**insalata mista**	*mixed salad*
bollito misto	*boiled meat*	**lingua**	*tongue*
bue	*beef*	**minestrone**	*vegetable soup*
carciofi	*artichokes*	**prosciutto**	*ham*
torta di		**polenta**	*maize or corn-*
frutta	*fruit tart*		*meal porridge*
fegato	*liver*	**pollo**	*chicken*
filetto	*fillet steak*	**pomodori**	*tomatoes*
	(tenderloin)	**risotto**	*rice*
fragole	*strawberries*	**trota**	*trout*
formaggio	*cheese*	**uova(e)**	*egg(s)*
funghi	*mushrooms*	**vitello**	*veal*

TIME DIFFERENCES   T

Like most of the Continent, Switzerland is on Central European
Time (GMT + 1). In summer the clock is put ahead one hour
(GMT + 2). In winter the time difference looks like this:

New York	London	**Switzerland**	Jo'burg	Sydney	Auckland
6 a.m.	11 a.m.	**noon**	1 p.m.	10 p.m.	midnight

TIPPING

In Swiss hotels and restaurants a service charge is included and
tipping has officially been phased out, but if the service has been
especially good, an extra franc or two is appropriate and appreciated. Porters, on the other hand, should be given 1 or 2 francs per
bag. As for taxis, in many cities the tip is included in the fare, and so
announced on a sign inside the cab; otherwise a 15% tip is
appropriate.

TOILETS

Throughout Switzerland you'll find clean public toilets at convenient
locations. Toilets are marked by conventional symbols for men and
women, or the expressions *Toiletten/toilettes/gabinetti* or *WC*.
Otherwise, women should look for the signs *Damen* or *Frauen* in
German, *dames* in French or *signore* or *donne* in Italian, and men for

Herren or *Männer* in German, *messieurs* in French, *signori* or *uomini* in Italian.

Where are the toilets?	Wo sind die Toiletten?	Où sont les toilettes?	Dove sono i gabinetti?

TOURIST INFORMATION OFFICES

In major cities abroad the Swiss National Tourist Office maintains representatives who provide complete information to help you plan your holiday.

Canada: Commerce Court West, Suite 2015 (P.O. Box 215), Toronto, Ont. M5L 1E8; tel. (416) 868-0584

South Africa: Agency with Swissair. Swiss House, 86 Main Street, P.O. Box 3866, Johannesburg; tel. (011) 836-9941

United Kingdom: Swiss Centre, 1 New Coventry Street, London W1V 8EE; tel. (01) 734-1921

U.S.A.: The Swiss Center, 608 Fifth Avenue, New York, NY 10020; tel. (212) 757-5944
250 Stockton Street, San Francisco, CA 94108; tel. (415) 362-2260

In Switzerland itself the head branch of the National Tourist Office *(Schweizerische Verkehrszentrale,* abbreviated *SVZ)* is at Bellariastrasse 38, 8027 Zurich; tel. (01) 202 37 37.

Almost every Swiss town or resort has its own autonomous tourist office well stocked with free brochures and booklets, local hotel lists and other information about the town itself and often other parts of the country as well. Among the larger offices:

Zurich: Bahnhofplatz 15 (Main Railway Station); tel. (01) 211 40 00

Basle: Blumenrain 2; tel. (061) 25 38 11

Berne: Central Railway Station; tel. (031) 22 76 76

Lucerne: Pilatusstrasse 14; tel. (041) 23 52 52

Geneva: Rue de la Tour-de-l'Ile 1; tel. (022) 28 72 33

Lausanne: Avenue d'Ouchy 60; tel. (021) 27 73 21

Bellinzona: Piazza Nosetto; tel. (092) 25 70 56

Where's the tourist office?	Wo ist das Verkehrsbüro?	Où est l'office du tourisme?	Dov'è l'ufficio turistico?

USEFUL EXPRESSIONS

English	German	French	Italian
good morning/afternoon	guten Tag	bonjour	buongiorno
good evening	guten Abend	bonsoir	buona sera
goodnight	gute Nacht	bonne nuit	buona notte
goodbye	auf Wiedersehen	au revoir	arrivederci
yes/no	ja/nein	oui/non	sì/no
please/thank you	bitte/danke	s'il vous plaît/merci	per favore/grazie
excuse me	Entschuldigung	pardon	scusi
you're welcome	bitte	pas de quoi	prego
where/when/how	wo/wann/wie	où/quand/comment	dove/quando/come
yesterday	gestern	hier	ieri
today	heute	aujourd'hui	oggi
tomorrow	morgen	demain	domani
day/week	Tag/Woche	jour/semaine	giorno/settimana
month/year	Monat/Jahr	mois/année	mese/anno
left/right	links/rechts	gauche/droite	sinistra/destra
up/down	oben/unten	en haut/en bas	su/giù
good/bad	gut/schlecht	bon/mauvais	buono/cattivo
big/small	gross/klein	grand/petit	grande/piccolo
cheap/expensive	billig/teuer	bon marché/cher	a buon mercato/caro
hot/cold	heiss/kalt	chaud/froid	caldo/freddo
old/new	alt/neu	vieux/neuf	vecchio/nuovo
open/closed	offen/geschlossen	ouvert/fermé	aperto/chiuso
free/occupied	frei/besetzt	libre/occupé	libero/occupato
early/late	früh/spät	tôt/tard	presto/tardi
easy/difficult	einfach/schwierig	facile/difficile	facile/difficile
Help me, please.	Helfen Sie mir, bitte.	Aidez moi, s'il vous plaît.	Mi aiuti, per favore.
How much is that?	Wieviel kostet das?	C'est combien?	Quant'è?
What time is it?	Wie spät ist es?	Quelle heure est-il?	Che ore sono?
I'd like...	Ich möchte...	J'aimerais...	Vorrei...

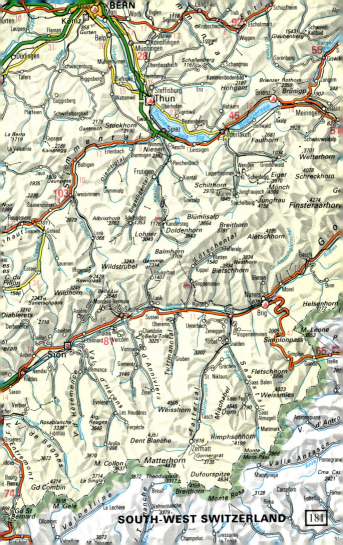

SOUTH-WEST SWITZERLAND

181

SOUTH-EAST SWITZERLAND p. 183

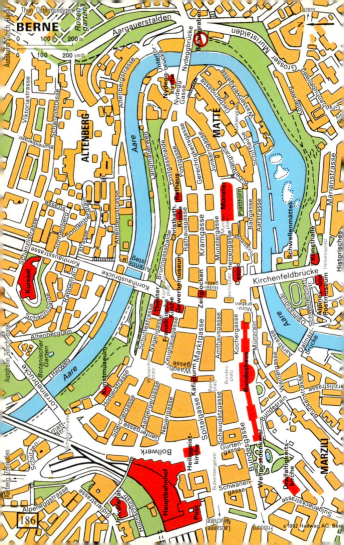

INDEX

An asterisk (*) next to a page number indicates a map reference. Where there is more than one set of page references, the one in bold type refers to the main entry. For index to Practical Information, see pages 152–153.